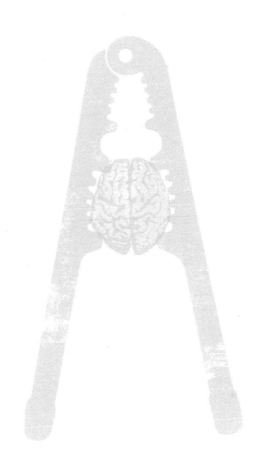

Infuriating Lateral Thinking
P U Z Z L E S

Paul Sloane & Des MacHale

PUZZLE
WRIGHT
PRESS

An imprint of Sterling
Publishing Co., Inc.
www.puzzlewright.com

Puzzlewright Press and the distinctive Puzzlewright Press logo are registered trademarks of
Sterling Publishing Co., Inc.

Library of Congress Cataloging-in-Publication Data Available

Illustrated by Myron Miller

The puzzles in this book originally appeared in
Intriguing Lateral Thinking Puzzles © 1996 by Paul Sloane and Des MacHale and
Perplexing Lateral Thinking Puzzles © 1997 by Paul Sloane and Des MacHale

2   4   6   8   10   9   7   5   3   1

Published by Sterling Publishing Co., Inc.
387 Park Avenue South, New York, NY 10016
© 2010 by Sterling Publishing Co., Inc.
Distributed in Canada by Sterling Publishing
^c/o Canadian Manda Group, 165 Dufferin Street,
Toronto, Ontario, Canada M6K 3H6

Manufactured in the United States of America
All rights reserved

Sterling ISBN 978-1-4027-6975-7

For information about custom editions, special sales, premium and
corporate purchases, please contact Sterling Special Sales
Department at 800-805-5489 or specialsales@sterlingpublishing.com.

Acknowledgments

We would like to acknowledge the input and inspiration of many people, including those too numerous to mention by name from all over the world, who have written to us with ideas and encouragement. Also to the contributors to the rec.puzzles newsgroup on the Internet who have given comments and feedback on some early ideas for this book.

This book could not have been produced without the help in editing and reviewing provided by Ann, Jackie, Hannah, and Val Sloane.

Contents

. . . .

Introduction

If you have seen this kind of puzzle before, you will know that it consists of strange situations that require an explanation. They are designed as a form of game for a small group, where one person knows the answer and the others try to figure it out by asking questions. The questions can only be answered by yes, no, or irrelevant. The puzzles can also be used as a form of training because they test and encourage skills in questioning, imagination, inductive reasoning, and lateral thinking.

Sure, some of the situations are implausible. And sure, it is possible to come up with alternative solutions that fit the original puzzle. In fact, you can play a variation of the game where people try to think of as many alternative explanations as possible. But in general, you will get the most enjoyment from these puzzles if you keep questioning until you come up with the answer given in the book. There is a clues section to help out when you get stuck, but the best resource is always your own imagination.

The Puzzles

The Late Report

A man and his wife went on vacation. Two months later, the man called the police to report the location of a body near the place where he had been on holiday. The police thanked the man and then asked why it had taken him two months to report the body. What was the reason?

Clues on p. 90/Answer on p. 142

The Stranger in the Bar

Two men went out for a drink together in a bar. One of them looked up, saw a tall, dark stranger looking like death and drinking soda water, and pointed him out to his companion. Startled and uneasy, the two men left and went to another bar some miles away. After a few minutes, they looked up and saw the same sad, pale stranger drinking soda water. Deciding to leave, they went to a third bar, which was empty except for a young couple. However, within a few minutes, the cadaverous man appeared and, in a slow, sad voice, ordered a soda water. Almost out of his mind, one of the men went over to him and said, "Who are you and what do you want?" What did the man answer?

Clues on p. 90/Answer on p. 142

Gertrude

When Gertrude entered the plane she caused her own death and the deaths of 200 people. Yet she was never blamed or criticized for her actions. What happened?

Clues on p. 90/Answer on p. 142

Mad Cow Ideas

In 1996, the British government was faced with the task of slaughtering many thousands of healthy cattle in order to allay fears over the disease BSE, or mad cow disease. What proposal did the government of Cambodia make to help solve the problem?

Clues on p. 90/Answer on p. 142

February 1866

What happened in February 1866 that will not happen again for another two and a half million years?

Clues on p. 91/Answer on p. 143

The Cabbie's Revenge

An American tourist in London took a taxi cab. When he reached his destination, the tourist paid the taxi driver the fare, but did not include a tip. The taxi driver was displeased and said something to the American that ruined his whole evening. The two men were strangers and had never met previously. What did the cabbie say?

Clues on p. 91/Answer on p. 143

Where in the World?

In what place would you find Julius Caesar, the biblical Rachel, King David, Pallas Athena (the Goddess of War), King Charlemagne, Alexander the Great, Queen Elizabeth I of England, and Sir Lancelot all together?

Clues on p. 91/Answer on p. 143

Scout's Honor

A boy scout was anxious to win maximum points at his monthly inspection. However, despite his mother's best efforts, she could not remove some blue felt-tip marker stains from his hands. What did she do?

Clues on p. 92/Answer on p. 143

The King's Favor

When King Charles II of England visited a College at the University of Cambridge, he noticed a fine portrait of his father, King Charles I, hanging in the Main Hall. He asked if he could have it, but the ruling body of the College was very reluctant to part with it. At last the King said that he would grant the College anything in his power if they would give him the portrait, and that he would be very displeased and unhelpful if they declined this generous offer. The College elders accepted. What did they ask for in return?

Clues on p. 92/Answer on p. 143

Price Tag

Many shops have prices set just under a round figure, e.g., $9.99 instead of $10 or $99.95 instead of $100. It is assumed that this is done because the price seems lower to the consumer, but this is not the reason the practice started. What was the original reason for this pricing method?

Clues on p. 92/Answer on p. 144

Color-Blind

John was color-blind. Because of this affliction, he landed an important job. What was it?

Clues on p. 92/Answer on p. 144

Seaside Idea

A military commander during World War II was on leave so he took his children to the seaside for a day. Here, he got the idea he needed in order to successfully carry out his next assignment. What was the idea?

Clues on p. 93/Answer on p. 144

The Hammer

Adam was jealous of Brenda's use of a computer. He changed that by means of a hammer. After that, he could use the computer, but Brenda could not. What did he do?

Clues on p. 93/Answer on p. 144

The Stranger in the Hotel

A woman was sitting in her hotel room when there was a knock at the door. She opened the door to see a man whom she had never seen before. He said, "Oh, I'm sorry. I have made a mistake. I thought this was my room." He then went off down the corridor to the elevator. The woman went back into her room and phoned reception to ask them to apprehend the man, who she was sure was a thief. What made her so sure?

Clues on p. 93/Answer on p. 145

Buttons

There is a reason why men's clothes have buttons on the right while women's have buttons on the left. What is it?

Clues on p. 93/Answer on p. 145

Upstairs, Downstairs

In a very exclusive restaurant several dozen diners are eating a top-class meal upstairs. Downstairs, precisely the same meal is being served at the same number of empty places where there is nobody to eat it. What is going on?

Clues on p. 93/Answer on p. 145

Inner Ear

An insect flying into a girl's ear terrifies her. Her mother rushes the girl to the doctor, but he is unable to remove the insect. Suddenly, the mother has an idea. What is it?

Clues on p. 94/Answer on p. 145

Inspired Composition

A composer of music sat looking out of a window, hoping for inspiration. Suddenly something he saw provided him with the opening theme for a new work. What did he see?

Clues on p. 94/Answer on p. 146

Early Morning in Las Vegas

A gambler went to Las Vegas. He won on the roulette table, lost at blackjack, and won at poker. When he went to bed in his hotel room, he carefully double-locked his door. At 3 a.m. he was awakened by the sound of someone banging and rattling on the door of his room. What did the person want, and what did the gambler do?

Clues on p. 94/Answer on p. 146

Large Number

Assume there are approximately 5,000,000,000 (5 billion) people on earth. What would you estimate to be the result, if you multiply together the number of fingers on every person's left hands? (For the purposes of this exercise, thumbs count as fingers, for five fingers per hand.) If you cannot estimate the number, then try to guess how long the number would be.

Clues on p. 94/Answer on p. 146

Souper

A woman was at an expensive and prestigious dinner. The first course was soup. Halfway through the course, she called over a waiter and whispered in his ear. He brought a drinking straw which she used to finish her soup. The other guests were surprised at her actions, but she had a good explanation. What was it?

Clues on p. 95/Answer on p. 146

The Single Flower

A woman was shown into a large room which contained over a thousand flowers. She was told that all but one of the flowers were artificial. She had to identify the real flower, but she could not examine the flowers closely nor smell them. She was alone in the room. What did she do to identify the single flower?

Clues on p. 95/Answer on p. 147

Unseen

As far as it is possible to ascertain, there is one thing which only one man in recorded history has not seen. All other men who have sight have seen it. The man was not blind and lived to a ripe old age. What was it that he never saw and how come?

Clues on p. 95/Answer on p. 147

The Champion's Blind Spot

At the dinner to celebrate the end of the Wimbledon tennis championship, the men's singles winner turned to the man next to him and said, "There is something here which you can see and all the other men can see but which I cannot see." What was it?

Clues on p. 95/Answer on p. 148

The Task

Several people are waiting to perform a task which they usually do by themselves very easily. Now, however, they are all in need of the services of someone who usually performs the task only with difficulty. What is going on?

Clues on p. 96/Answer on p. 148

WALLY Test I

From the World Association for Learning, Laughter and Youth (WALLY) comes another quickfire WALLY test. It consists of mean questions designed to trip you up. Test your wits now by writing down the answers to these questions. You have two minutes to complete the test.

1. There were eight ears of corn in a hollow stump. A squirrel can carry out three ears a day. How many days does it take the squirrel to take all the ears of corn from the stump?
2. Which triangle is larger—one with sides measuring 200, 300, and 400 cm or one with sides measuring 300, 400, and 700 cm?
3. How far can a dog run into a wood?
4. Which of the following animals would see best in total darkness: an owl, a leopard, or an eagle?
5. What was the highest mountain in the world before Mount Everest was discovered?
6. Where are the Kings and Queens of England crowned?
7. If the vice president of the U.S. were killed, who would then become president?
8. Which candles burn longer—beeswax or tallow?
9. A farmer had 4 haystacks in one field and twice as many in each of his other two fields. He put the haystacks from all three fields together. How many haystacks did he now have?
10. What five-letter word becomes shorter when you add two letters to it?
11. Which weighs more—a pound of feathers or a pound of gold?
12. What has four legs and only one foot?

Answers on p. 190

What a Jump!

A man jumped 150 feet entirely under his own power. He landed safely. How did he do it?

Clues on p. 96/Answer on p. 148

The String and the Cloth

A man lay dead in a field next to a piece of string and a cloth. How did he die?

Clues on p. 96/Answer on p. 148

A Riddle

Four men sat down to play.
They played all night till break of day.
They played for gold and not for fun,
With separate scores for everyone.
When they came to square accounts
They all made quite fair amounts.
Can you this paradox explain?
If no one lost, how could all gain?

Clues on p. 96/Answer on p. 148

Bad Impression

A man entered a city art gallery and did terrible damage to some very valuable Impressionist paintings. Later that day, instead of being arrested, he was thanked by the curator of the art gallery for his actions. How come?

Clues on p. 97/Answer on p. 149

The Animal

At the Carlton Club, Alan Quartermaine was telling one of his stories. "When the animal emerged from the lake I could see that its four knees were wet," he said. Marmaduke, who had walked into the room at that very point, then interrupted, "I know what kind of an animal that was." How did he know, and what kind of animal was it?

Clues on p. 97/Answer on p. 149

Escape

A man was trapped on an island in the middle of a large and deep lake. He could not swim and had no boat or means of making one. He waited desperately for help, but none came. Eventually he managed to escape. How?

Clues on p. 97/Answer on p. 149

Poisoned

A man is found dead in a locked room. He has died of poisoning, and it looks like suicide. No one was with him when he took the poison, but it was, in fact, murder. How come?

Clues on p. 97/Answer on p. 149

Failed Forgery

A master forger forged a U.S. $100 bill. The bills he made were perfect copies of the original in every detail, yet he was caught. How?

Clues on p. 98/Answer on p. 149

Apprehended

Some time ago a burglar ransacked a house in the middle of the night and left without anybody seeing him, yet the police picked him up within a few hours. How did they trace him?

Clues on p. 98/Answer on p. 150

The Metal Ball

. . . .

At the beginning of his act, a magician places a solid metal ball, 4 inches in diameter, on a table and places a cover over it. At the end of his act when he lifts the cover, the ball has disappeared. How?

Clues on p. 98/Answer on p. 150

One Croaked!

. . . .

Two frogs fell into a large cylindrical tank of liquid and both fell to the bottom. The walls were sheer and slippery. One frog died but one survived. How?

Clues on p. 98/Answer on p. 150

Unspoken Understanding

A deaf-and-dumb man went into a subway. He walked up to the cashier's booth and gave the cashier a dollar. The subway tokens cost 40 cents each. The cashier gave the man two tokens. Not a word was said, nor any sign given. How did the cashier know that the man indeed wanted two tokens?

Clues on p. 98/Answer on p. 150

His Widow's Sister

It was reported in the paper that Jim Jones had married his widow's sister. How did he do this?

Clues on p. 99/Answer on p. 150

Light Years Ahead

If you could travel faster than the speed of light, then you could catch up with the light which radiated from your body some time ago. You would then be able to see yourself as you used to be when you were younger. Although faster-than-light travel is impossible, at least at this time, how can we catch up with the light that we radiated earlier and see ourselves directly—as we used to be? (Such captured images as photographs, movies, and videotape do not count.)

Clues on p. 99/Answer on p. 151

The Newspaper

Jim and Joe were fighting, so their mother punished them by making them both stand on the same sheet of yesterday's newspaper until they were ready to make up. She did this in such a way that neither of the boys could touch the other. How did she manage to do this?

Clues on p. 100/Answer on p. 151

Light Work

There are 3 light switches outside a room. They are connected to three light bulbs inside the room. Each switch can be in the on position or the off position. You are allowed to set the switches and then to enter the room once. You then have to determine which switch is connected to which bulb. How do you do it?

Clues on p. 100/Answer on p. 151

What a Bore!

An office worker has a colleague in her office outstaying his welcome. She can see that he is not inclined to leave any time soon. Concerned about his feelings, how does she manage to get rid of him without offending him?

Clues on p. 100/Answer on p. 151

Soviet Pictures

During the dark days of the Soviet Union, purges took place following which experts in photography would doctor photographs to remove individuals who had been purged. How was one expert caught?

Clues on p. 100/Answer on p. 151

Penniless

A struggling author receives a present of $2,000 from a lady admirer. He does not tell his wife about this cash gift, although she has shared all his trials and is very supportive. How did she find out that he had received the money?

Clues on p. 101/Answer on p. 152

The Deadly Suitcase

A woman opened a suitcase and found to her horror that there was a body inside. How had it got there?

Clues on p. 101/Answer on p. 152

Unknown Character

A recluse who had lived for many years in a small community was charged with a serious crime. He knew nobody in the area. Whom did he call as a character witness?

Clues on p. 101/Answer on p. 152

Gasoline Problem

A man's car runs out of gasoline. His car tank holds exactly 13 gallons. He has three empty unmarked containers which can hold 3 gallons, 6 gallons, and 11 gallons. Using only these containers at the gas station, how can the man bring back exactly 13 gallons? He is not allowed to buy more than 13 gallons and dispose of the extra.

Clues on p. 101/Answer on p. 152

Poison Pen

A woman received a very nasty, anonymous letter containing threats and allegations. She called the police and they quickly found out who had sent it. How?

Clues on p. 101/Answer on p. 153

The Coconut Millionaire

A man buys coconuts at $5 a dozen and sells them at $3 a dozen. As a result of this he becomes a millionaire. How come?

Clues on p. 102/Answer on p. 153

The Music Stopped Again

When the music stopped, he died very suddenly. How?

Clues on p. 102/Answer on p. 153

Disreputable

A man was born before his father, killed his mother, and married his sister. Yet he was considered normal by all those who knew him. How come?

Clues on p. 102/Answer on p. 153

Personality Plus

An agency offered personality assessments on the basis of handwriting. How did an enterprising client show that the operation was unreliable?

Clues on p. 102/Answer on p. 153

Gambler's Ruin

Syd Sharp, a first-class card player, regularly won large amounts at poker. He was also excellent at bridge, blackjack, cribbage, canasta, and pinochle. Joe, on the other hand, was terrible at cards; he could never remember what had gone before or figure out what card to play next. One day, Joe challenged Syd to a game of cards for money. Over the next couple of hours, Joe proceeded to win quite a large amount from Syd. How?

Clues on p. 102/Answer on p. 154

WALLY Test II

Just when you thought you were safe—another WALLY test! Write down the answer to each question as soon as possible after reading it. You have two minutes to complete the test.

1. Which two whole numbers multiplied together make 17?

2. If post is spelled POST, and most is spelled MOST, how do you spell the word for what you put in the toaster?

3. What five-letter word contains six when two letters are taken away?

4. A Muslim living in England cannot be buried on Church ground even if he converts to Christianity. Why not?

5. How many bananas can a grown man eat on an empty stomach?

6. Why is it that Beethoven never finished the Unfinished Symphony?

7. What common word is pronounced wrongly by over half of all Yale and Harvard graduates?

8. What gets larger the more you take away?

9. If I gave you ten cents for every quarter you could stand on edge and you stood three quarters on their edge, how much money would you gain?

10. If there are 12 six-cent stamps in a dozen, then how many two-cent stamps are there in a dozen?

Answers on p. 190-191

Fast Work

When she was picked up, it was discovered that Marion had married ten men. They were all still alive, but no charges were pressed against her. Why not?

Clues on p. 103/Answer on p. 154

The Flicker

A man was running along a corridor clutching a piece of paper. He saw the lights flicker. He gave a cry of anguish and walked on dejectedly. Why?

Clues on p. 103/Answer on p. 154

An American Shooting

One American man shot another American man dead in full view of many people. The two men had never met before and did not know each other. Neither was a policeman nor a criminal. The man who shot and killed the other man was not arrested or charged with any crime. Why not?

Clues on p. 103/Answer on p. 154

King George

King George the Third of England suffered a temporary bout of madness. A movie was made in England on this subject. It was entitled "The Madness of George III," but this name was changed for American audiences. Why?

Clues on p. 103/Answer on p. 155

Fallen Angel

A butterfly fell down, and a man was seriously injured. Why?

Clues on p. 103/Answer on p. 155

The Flaw in the Carpet

A man bought a very expensive oriental carpet in a reputable carpet shop in a Middle Eastern country. After he had bought it, he found that it had a flaw. He took it back to the shop. It was agreed that there was a flaw in the carpet, but the shopkeeper refused to take back the carpet or give any kind of refund or reduction in price. Why not?

Clues on p. 103/Answer on p. 155

What a Relief!

Immediately after the end of World War II, a doctor in France approached a soldier who was perfectly healthy and asked for a large sample of his urine. Why was this?

Clues on p. 104/Answer on p. 155

First Choice

A travel article on Brazil observed that, in restaurants in Rio, soup was a very popular first course for rich ladies. Why?

Clues on p. 104/Answer on p. 156

Disturbance

A man went to his neighbor's house at 3 in the morning and started shouting and banging on the door. He would not stop until the neighbors opened the door and stood facing him. Initially angry, they later thanked the man. Why?

Clues on p. 104/Answer on p. 156

Mona Lisa

Why did a group of enterprising thieves steal the famous painting the Mona Lisa and then return it undamaged a few months later?

Clues on p. 104/Answer on p. 156

Snow Joy

Children in a town in New England were delighted one snowy January day. The snow was so heavy that school had to be canceled. Their joy continued when the deep snow caused the same thing to happen on the next few days. Then they became disappointed and upset at having to miss school. Why?

Clues on p. 105/Answer on p. 157

The Cheat

A man cheated a woman out of $5. When she found out, she killed him. They were not poor. Her defense lawyer argued that she was justified in her actions, and many people agreed with him. Why?

Clues on p. 105/Answer on p. 157

Dutch Race

One of the most prestigious races in Holland involves many people and enormous organization. But nobody knows when it will be held until two days before the race. Why?

Clues on p. 105/Answer on p. 157

Wino

A man was enjoying his meal at a dinner party and had just started a delicious dessert. Why did he deliberately knock over the salt shaker into his dessert and ruin it?

Clues on p. 105/Answer on p. 158

Garden Story

Why did a man tell his wife that he had buried guns in their garden when he knew that he had not?

Clues on p. 106/Answer on p. 158

Fireworks Display

A young family went out to a fireworks display. On their return, the parents were very sad. Why?

Clues on p. 106/Answer on p. 158

The Fallen Guide

A mountain climber in the Himalayas took along with him two mountain guides. After a few hours, one of the guides fell into a deep crevasse. The climber and the other guide continued the climb and did not raise the alarm. Why?

Clues on p. 106/Answer on p. 158

The Yacht Incident

A yacht is found floating in the middle of the ocean, and around it in the water are a dozen human corpses. Why?

Clues on p. 106/Answer on p. 158

Self-Addressed Envelope

Why does a man send himself a letter every day but Saturday?

Clues on p. 107/Answer on p. 159

Fingered

Why did a political candidate always place his finger on the chest of any man when he was canvassing them in public?

Clues on p. 107/Answer on p. 159

The Gross Grocery List

A woman handed a man a grocery list, but when he handed it back to her she was extremely embarrassed. Why?

Clues on p. 107/Answer on p. 159

Finger Break

Why did a woman take a baseball bat and break her husband's fingers?

Clues on p. 108/Answer on p. 159

Unpublished

An eminent firm of publishers had a manuscript for a novel. It was written by a very well-known author and was sure to sell well. However, they chose not to publish it. Why?

Clues on p. 108/Answer on p. 160

The Unwanted Gift

A nobleman was very displeased when he received an expensive gift from the King. Why?

Clues on p. 109/Answer on p. 160

Benjamin Franklin

Benjamin Franklin was a well-educated man. Why did he deliberately spell Philadelphia wrong?

Clues on p. 109/Answer on p. 160

Middle Eastern Muddle

One of the most successful advertising agencies in the U.S. acquired a Middle Eastern account. Their first ad there made them a laughingstock. Why?

Clues on p. 109/Answer on p. 161

The Wounded Soldier

A badly wounded but conscious soldier is brought into a field hospital during a battle. The surgeon takes a quick look at him and then says to the orderly, "Get this man out of here! He is a coward who has smeared himself with the blood of his comrades." Why did he say this?

Clues on p. 109/Answer on p. 161

Ice Rinked

A man skating at an ice rink saw a woman slip and fall. Although she was a stranger to him, he wanted to find out if she was all right. He went over to her, but before he said anything she slapped him hard across the face. They had never met or communicated before. Why did she strike him?

Clues on p. 109/Answer on p. 161

On Time

Why did a man who knew the time and had an accurate watch call information?

Clues on p. 110/Answer on p. 161

Cat Food

A man who did not like cats bought some fresh salmon and cream for a cat. Why?

Clues on p. 110/Answer on p. 162

Rich Man, Poor Man

A man making over $10 million a year drives a small car, lives in a modest house, and insists he can't afford luxuries. Why not?

Clues on p. 110/Answer on p. 162

Sleeping on the Job

A man undressed to go to bed and hundreds of people lost their jobs. Why?

Clues on p. 110/Answer on p. 162

Fine Art

An art collector went into the art dealer, Sotheby's. He asked to have two items valued. One was an old violin and the other an oil painting. The experts studied them for days before confirming their remarkable findings. The collector was told that the two items were an original Stradivarius and a previously unknown work by Vincent van Gogh. At first, the collector was thrilled but later he became very dejected. Why?

Clues on p. 110/Answer on p. 162

Ford's Lunch

Before hiring anyone in a senior post, Henry Ford, the auto magnate, always took the candidate out to dinner. Why?

Clues on p. 111/Answer on p. 163

The Hairdresser

A New York City hairdresser recently said that he would rather cut the hair of three Canadians than one New Yorker. Why?

Clues on p. 111/Answer on p. 163

Not a Hair

Lyndsey, an elegant fashion model and actor, was caught out in the rain one day during a photography session. Without hat or umbrella, she dashed through the rain for shelter. The strange thing was that not one hair on the model's head got wet. Why not?

Clues on p. 111/Answer on p. 163

The Plate of Mushrooms

A man enjoyed the taste of mushrooms but had a morbid fear of being poisoned by them, so he never ate them. Yet one day he ordered a large plate of assorted mushrooms to eat. Why?

Clues on p. 111/Answer on p. 163

Order Delayed

One night, a man staying in a small Tokyo hotel ordered a drink from room service. It never came. Early in the morning, he was awakened by a loud knock on his door. Why?

Clues on p. 111/Answer on p. 163

Silence Is Golden

A distinguished speaker once gave a very interesting talk to a packed and enthusiastic audience. However, after the talk finished there was no applause whatsoever. Why?

Clues on p. 112/Answer on p. 164

Bluebeard's Treasure

The pirate Bluebeard buried his treasure on a desert island. Some time later he heard that one of his enemies had obtained a copy of the map which showed the exact location of the treasure, but Bluebeard was not worried. Why not?

Clues on p. 112/Answer on p. 164

The King

A man is crowned King. Shortly afterwards, he is captured by enemy forces and chopped in two. Why?

Clues on p. 113/Answer on p. 164

Lockout

Jefferson Jones was an art collector with a valuable collection in his apartment. It had one door, and he fitted it with six locks. While he was away, a determined burglar who was skilled at picking locks tried to open the door, but although he could pick the locks he could not get in. Why not?

Clues on p. 113/Answer on p. 165

Creepy Crawly

On a trip deep in the Amazonian jungle, the explorer Alan Quartermaine woke one morning. He could feel something inside his sleeping bag. It had a head and a tail and it moved when he moved. However, he was calm and unafraid. Why?

Clues on p. 113/Answer on p. 165

The Unlucky Trip

A man hurried down an unlit road with a torch in his hand. He tripped and dropped the torch, which went out. No damage was done, and no one was was hurt, but the incident was reported in newspapers around the world. Why?

Clues on p. 113/Answer on p. 165

Checked

A man wrote out and signed a check from his own checkbook for $1,000. There was more than this in his account. Yet he was charged with fraud. Why?

Clues on p. 114/Answer on p. 165

Fruitless Search

A man was searching for blue-back frogs in an area where they were very common. He caught one. It started to rain, and he became frantic. The rain grew stronger, and the man left, disconsolate. Why?

Clues on p. 114/Answer on p. 165

Truckload

A fully loaded truck that weighs exactly 10 tons starts to cross a long bridge which at its center can carry a load of exactly 10 tons—no more. As he reaches the center the driver hears the bridge creak so he slows down. Just then, a flock of starlings lands on the roof of the truck but the bridge does not break. Why not?

Clues on p. 114/Answer on p. 166

The Deadly Melody

A woman heard a tune which she recognized. She took a gun and shot a stranger. Why?

Clues on p. 114/Answer on p. 166

The Sign

A man and his wife were in their car. The man saw a sign. Without either of them saying a word, he drew a gun and shot his wife dead. Why?

Clues on p. 115/Answer on p. 166

New Shoes

A woman bought a new pair of shoes and then went to work. She died. Why?

Clues on p. 115/Answer on p. 166

The Archduke
. . . .

When Archduke Ferdinand was shot in 1914, his attendants could not undo his coat to stem his bleeding wound. Why not?

Clues on p. 115/Answer on p. 167

The Hasty Packer
. . . .

She died because she packed too quickly. How did she die?

Clues on p. 115/Answer on p. 167

Heartless
. . . .

A man who was surrounded by other people suddenly had a heart attack. Everyone saw this, but no one intervened. He subsequently died. There was no ill-will towards him, and no physical barrier between him and the others. Why did no one try to help him?

Clues on p. 115/Answer on p. 167

Dead Drunk
. . . .

A man was coming home after a night out drinking. There was no one around, so he decided to relieve himself. Within minutes he was dead. What happened?

Clues on p. 116/Answer on p. 167

The Big Room

A man is lying dead in a big room. Musical instruments lie around. He is holding a bottle of brandy. He died because of the brandy, but how?

Clues on p. 116/Answer on p. 167

Sacrifice

Three castaways were starving on a desert island. When they had run out of food they decided that one of them had to die to be eaten by the other two. All three were single, of the same age, experience, size, and skills. But they easily decided who should die. How?

Clues on p. 116/Answer on p. 168

Stolen Finger

A man sneaked into a morgue one night and cut the little finger off a corpse. Why?

Clues on p. 116/Answer on p. 168

Poor Dogs

During World War II, why did German soldiers have to shoot the dogs they had carefully trained?

Clues on p. 117/Answer on p. 168

Radio Death

A man is driving his car. He turns on the radio and hears music. He stops and shoots himself. Why?

Clues on p. 117/Answer on p. 169

Thirsty

A man dies of thirst in his own home. How come?

Clues on p. 117/Answer on p. 169

Aftershave

A man is given a bottle of aftershave for his birthday. He puts some on and later that day he dies. How?

Clues on p. 117/Answer on p. 169

Capsize

A riverboat in good condition is steaming down a calm river when it suddenly capsizes, drowning most of the passengers. What happened?

Clues on p. 117/Answer on p. 169

Untying the Ropes

When they untied the ropes, everyone knew he was dead. How?

Clues on p. 118/Answer on p. 170

Murder in the Newspaper

An old man read a report in his morning newspaper about a wealthy woman who had died of old age. "She was murdered!" he gasped. Then he carried on reading the rest of the newspaper. How did he know that it was murder, and why did he do nothing about it?

Clues on p. 118/Answer on p. 170

The Man Who Returned Too Soon

One bright sunny morning a man left his home. After some time he decided to return home and came back straightaway. When he got home, he died. If he had not gone home so quickly, he would have lived. What happened?

Clues on p. 118/Answer on p. 170

The Truck Driver

A truck driver was driving along an empty highway, when he sensed there was something wrong with his truck. He stopped and got out to look at it. He was then killed. How?

Clues on p. 119/Answer on p. 170

The Circle and the Line

They died because the circle crossed the line. Explain.

Clues on p. 119/Answer on p. 171

The Perfect Murder

Edward carefully plotted the murder of his wife. One winter's day he strangled her in the bedroom, then faked a burglary. He ransacked the house, scattered possessions, and broke through the patio doors. He set the burglar alarm downstairs before driving to the local golf course to establish his alibi. Two hours later, when Edward was in the middle of his golf game with three colleagues, the burglar alarm went off and the police were alerted. They found the house apparently broken into and the wife strangled. No animals or electrical devices were found which could have set the alarm off, so it looked as though an intruder had set off the alarm before killing the poor woman. Edward was never arrested or charged. The police inspector long suspected Edward, but there was one question which he could not fathom: How did the suspect get the burglar alarm to go off so conveniently? Can you work it out?

Clues on p. 119/Answer on p. 171

The Sniper

A man is driving in a war zone when he is attacked by a sniper. His car skids and turns over. He manages to crawl out and get behind his car, but he is still under fire from the sniper. He has no gun. All he has is a bottle of water, a handkerchief, and a cigarette lighter. How does he escape?

Clues on p. 119/Answer on p. 171

Fair Deal

Several truck drivers at a roadside café started to play poker. The pot was large, and the game was serious. Suddenly one of the men accused the dealer of cheating. The dealer drew a knife and, in plain view of all the others, stabbed the man and killed him. The police were called, and they interviewed everyone who had been present, but no man was arrested or charged with any offense. Why not?

Clues on p. 120/Answer on p. 171

The Cloth

A man waved a cloth and another man died. Why?

Clues on p. 120/Answer on p. 172

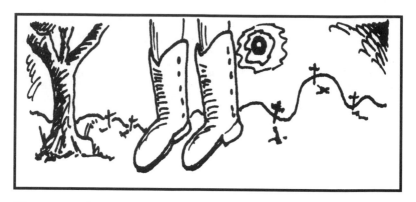

Bostonian

A man was born in Boston, Massachusetts. Both his parents were born in Boston, Massachusetts. He lived all his life in Boston, but he was not a United States citizen. How come?

Clues on p. 120/Answer on p. 172

The Tree and the Axe

A woman bought a young tree and put it in her garden. The next day she took an axe to it. Why?

Clues on p. 120/Answer on p. 172

Below Par

A middle-aged man took up golf for the first time, and within a month he went around his local course in under 90 shots. However, he was not pleased. Why?

Clues on p. 120/Answer on p. 172

School Friend

Joe went back to his hometown and met an old school friend he had not seen for years. His friend said, "I am married now but not to anyone you know. This is my daughter."

Joe turned to the little girl and asked her her name. She said, "I have the same name as my mother."

"Then you must be called Louise," said Joe. He was right, but how did he know?

Clues on p. 121/Answer on p. 172

Sell More Beer

A management consultant went into a bar one evening. After a little while he told the bar owner a simple and quite legal way of selling a lot more beer. However, the bar owner was not pleased. Why not?

Clues on p. 121/Answer on p. 172

The Lumberjacks

Tim and Joe are two lumberjacks who work at the same rate of speed. One morning, Tim works steadily from 8 o'clock to noon without taking a break. Joe starts and finishes at the same time, but he takes a five-minute break every half-hour. At the end of the period Joe has felled considerably more trees than Tim. How come?

Clues on p. 121/Answer on p. 172

The Clinch

A prim lady was disgusted that the teenage boy and girl in front of her at the cinema remained locked in a passionate embrace throughout the entire feature. She called the manager, who immediately summoned an ambulance. Why?

Clues on p. 121/Answer on p. 173

Precognition

A lady knocked at the door of a tiny cottage and when an old lady opened the door she said, "Good morning, Mrs. Turner." Neither of them had ever met, nor seen or heard of the other before. How did she know the old lady's name?

Clues on p. 121/Answer on p. 173

Dud Car

The Chevrolet Nova was a successful car in many countries but not in Mexico. Why not?

Clues on p. 122/Answer on p. 173

Red Light

A police officer was sitting on his motorcycle at a red traffic light when two teenagers in a sports car drove by him at 50 miles per hour. He did not chase them or try to apprehend them. Why not?

Clues on p. 122/Answer on p. 173

Nun-plussed

A priest sitting in a doctor's waiting room was horrified to see a crying nun, rushing from the doctor's surgery, followed by a flustered doctor. Angrily he asked the doctor for an explanation. What explanation did the doctor give?

Clues on p. 122/Answer on p. 173

Confectionery Manufacturer

A manufacturer of confectionery has a work force of thousands of workers. They never strike or demand better conditions. They work up to twenty hours per day and receive no wages except food and shelter. Yet every year a completely new work force is brought in and none of the existing workers is re-employed. Why?

Clues on p. 122/Answer on p. 173

The Painter

Much of his painting was seen at the city's two large art galleries but no one had ever heard of him. Why not?

Clues on p. 122/Answer on p. 173

Regular Arguments

Every evening a man and a woman would eat at a table and then have a violent argument, swearing, shouting, and insulting each other. The rest of the time they got on very well, with never a cross word. Why did they argue every night?

Clues on p. 123/Answer on p. 174

Beautiful Girls

As a group of sailors emerged from their ship after months at sea, one spindly wimp bet his fellow sailors that he would have a beautiful girl on each arm within an hour. How did he win his bet?

Clues on p. 123/Answer on p. 174

Orange Trick

There is an orange in the middle of a circular table. Without touching or moving the orange or the table how could you place a second orange under the first?

Clues on p. 123/Answer on p. 174

The Fall

A man fell 140 feet without a parachute. He turned upside-down seven times and came to land safely on solid ground. How come?

Clues on p. 123/Answer on p. 174

The Bookmark

A man who needs a bookmark is offered a fine bookmark for a dollar. Why does he refuse it?

Clues on p. 123/Answer on p. 174

Good-bye, Mother

A young woman in a restaurant was approached by a tearful old lady who said, "You look so much like my own daughter who passed away last year. Could you do me a favor and say 'Good-bye, Mother' when I leave?"

The young woman happily agreed and said, "Good-bye, Mother" when the old lady left. Later she got a shock. What was it?

Clues on p. 123/Answer on p. 174

Steer Clear of the Banks

A man drove into town and parked at the end of the main street. He got out of his car and went up to the bookstore at the opposite end of the street. He then came back down the street to his car and drove off. There are three banks on the main street, but the man did not walk past any of them. Why not?

Clues on p. 124/Answer on p. 174

A Hairy Story

A man who was completely bald met a doctor at a party. She had lovely short black hair. He explained that he had tried hair restorers and transplants but without any success. She sympathized. "If you could make my hair look like yours, I would gladly pay you $1,000," he said.

"O.K., I'll do it," she answered. How did she win the $1,000?

Clues on p. 124/Answer on p. 175

By the River

A police officer saw a man standing by a river holding a loaded gun near his head. The officer rushed towards the man and grabbed the gun. A minute later he handed the gun back with apologies. Why?

Clues on p. 124/Answer on p. 175

WALLY Test III

Sharpen your pencil and your wits! Here comes a WALLY Test. Write out your answers to these quickfire questions:

1. In Camberley, England, two out of every seven people have telephone numbers that are not listed in the directory. If there are 14,000 names in the Camberley telephone directory, how many of them have numbers that are unlisted?

2. In Iran, a Westerner cannot take a photograph of a man with a turban. Why not?

3. How many successful parachute jumps does a trainee parachutist in the U.S. Army have to make before he graduates from jump school?

4. What is the invention, first discovered in ancient times, that allows people to see through solid walls?

5. A man carefully pointed his car due east and then drove for two miles. He was then two miles west of where he started from. How come?

6. A mail plane was halfway from Dallas to Miami at a height of 2,000 feet on a clear, still day. It dropped a 100 kg sack of airmail letters and a 100 kg steel rod at the same time. Which hit the ground first?

7. If two are company and three are a crowd, what are four and five?

8. With which hand does a nun stir her coffee?

9. Why do some people press elevator buttons with their fingers and others with their thumbs?

10. What do you say to a man who claims not to be superstitious?

11. If a grandfather clock strikes thirteen, what time is it?

12. Two sons, two fathers, and a grandfather sat together. How many men were there?

13. An archaeologist showed his daughter a coin that he had found on a dig. He told her it was dated 200 BC. She told him she thought it was a fake. Who was right?

14. For this two-parter, tell us: a) What color is a refrigerator? b) What do cows drink?

Answers on p. 191

The Helicopter

A helicopter was hovering 200 feet above the sea when the pilot suddenly turned off the engine. The rotor stopped, but the helicopter did not crash. Why not?

Clues on p. 125/Answer on p. 175

Car in the River

A man was driving alone in his car when he spun off the road at high speed. He crashed through a fence and bounced down a steep ravine before the car plunged into a fast-flowing river. As the car slowly settled in the river, the man realized that his arm was broken and that he could not release his seat belt and get out of the car. The car sank to the bottom of the river. He was trapped in the car. Rescuers arrived two hours later, yet they found him alive. How come?

Clues on p. 125/Answer on p. 175

Pay Phone

A lady depended on a pay phone to make calls but it was frequently out of order. Each day she reported the problem to the telephone company but nothing was done. Finally, she phoned the company with a false piece of information which caused the telephone to be fixed within hours. What did she tell them?

Clues on p. 125/Answer on p. 175

The Typist

A young woman applied for a job as a secretary and typist. There were dozens of applicants. The woman could type only eleven words per minute, yet she got the job. Why?

Clues on p. 125/Answer on p. 175

Two Jugs

A man had a jug full of lemonade and a jug full of milk. He poured them both into one large vat, yet he kept the lemonade separate from the milk. How?

Clues on p. 126/Answer on p. 175

Speeding Ticket

A man is driving his car at ten miles an hour down a quiet suburban street when a police officer spots him and fines him for speeding. Why?

Clues on p. 126/Answer on p. 176

Twin Trouble

Bob and Sam were identical twins born in London in 1911. Bob was born before Sam, but Sam was older than Bob. How come?

Clues on p. 126/Answer on p. 176

Library Lunacy

A public library suddenly announced that each member could borrow up to ten books and not return them for up to six months. Why?

Clues on p. 126/Answer on p. 176

Elevator

A woman was in an elevator. She was frightened. She sat down. She laughed and stood up. Why?

Clues on p. 127/Answer on p. 176

Fall of the Wall

In its day, the Great Wall of China was considered virtually impregnable, yet it was breached within a few years of being built. How?

Clues on p. 127/Answer on p. 176

Smart Appearance

Victor was smartly dressed, well-shaven, and with the best haircut he had had for years. Many of his friends and relatives saw him, yet no one complimented him. Why not?

Clues on p. 127/Answer on p. 177

Dogs Home

A boy brings home a lost puppy, but his parents order him to dispose of it. As he walks into town, wondering what to do, he sees a truck with Dogs Home printed on it. He slips the puppy into the truck, but this leads to a minor disaster. Why?

Clues on p. 127/Answer on p. 177

Title Role

A vain actress was thrilled to hear from her agent that she had received the title role in the movie of a famous book. But later she was very displeased. Why?

Clues on p. 127/Answer on p. 177

Job Lot

A builder was very pleased to buy a job lot of bricks at a very low price. When he examined them he found that they were sound, strong, and well-made, but he was extremely unhappy. Why?

Clues on p. 128/Answer on p. 177

The Lifeboat

A man was cast adrift in a lifeboat. He was horrified to see that it was letting in water, so he diligently bailed out the water. After two days, he did not bother bailing out the water anymore. Why not?

Clues on p. 128/Answer on p. 177

Invaluable

A man got something of little value. It became very valuable so he threw it away. If it had been worth less, he would have kept it. Why?

Clues on p. 128/Answer on p. 178

The Crash

In heavy fog, there was a serious accident which involved two trucks and six cars. All the vehicles were severely damaged. Police and ambulances were quickly on the scene, where they found both truck drivers and took them to the hospital for treatment. However, no drivers from any of the cars could be found at the scene of the accident. Why not?

Clues on p. 128/Answer on p. 178

Westward Ho!

(West) Bristol ————— Reading ————— London (East)

Two men set off on foot one morning. They started from Reading and headed east towards London. They walked until they reached a restaurant, where they sat down and had lunch. They then carried on walking east towards London. They arrived that same afternoon in Bristol. Since the only direction in which they walked was east, how was it possible for them to arrive in Bristol?

Clues on p. 128/Answer on p. 178

40 Feet Ahead

A man set out for a walk. At the end of his walk, his head had travelled 40 feet farther than his feet had travelled. He was a healthy man with all his limbs intact before and after the walk. So how did his head travel farther than his feet?

Clues on p. 129/Answer on p. 179

The Circular Table

A lady has an expensive, circular, oak table and she wishes to find its exact center. How does she do this without marking the table in any way?

Clues on p. 129/Answer on p. 179

T-Shirts

A change in the law in Italy resulted in large sales of white T-shirts with black bands on them. How come?

Clues on p. 130/Answer on p. 179

Two Suitcases

A man is carrying two suitcases, one in each hand. One is a big empty suitcase. The other is a smaller, light suitcase full of books. He puts the smaller suitcase into the bigger one, making it heavy and difficult to carry. Why does he do this?

Clues on p. 130/Answer on p. 180

The Nonchalant Police Officer

One fine morning, a police officer was walking down the high street in the middle of town. Turning a corner, he gasped as he saw two armed robbers dash out of a bank, firing guns as they left. He then ignored them, and continued walking up the street. Why?

Clues on p. 130/Answer on p. 180

Rare Event

What happened in the second half of the 20th century and will not happen again for over 4,000 years?

Clues on p. 130/Answer on p. 180

Holy Orders

A priest goes into a church carrying a loaded gun. Why?

Clues on p. 131/Answer on p. 180

Well-Dressed

Why did the lady always answer the door wearing her hat and coat?

Clues on p. 131/Answer on p. 180

Kid Stuff

Many more children are involved as pedestrians in road accidents than might be expected from their numbers and road use. An expert on road accidents has put forward an ingenious theory to account for this. What do you think the theory might be?

Clues on p. 131/Answer on p. 181

The Two Drivers

Two drivers drove slowly and safely in the correct direction down a wide road before coming to a stop in front of a red stoplight. A nearby police officer immediately arrested one of the drivers and let the other one drive off. The police officer had never seen or heard of either driver before. Neither driver had a criminal record. They were both fully dressed and no one had been drinking. Both cars were in excellent condition and had not been stolen. The arrested driver was charged and convicted. Of what?

Clues on p. 131/Answer on p. 181

Keys in the Car

A man locks his keys inside his car and is unable to get them out despite trying for an hour. A police officer comes by and offers to help. He discovers that the back door of the car is unlocked, and he recovers the keys. The man thanks him, but when the officer departs the man locks the keys back inside. Why?

Clues on p. 132/Answer on p. 181

The Hasty Robber

A man robbed a bank. If he had seen the other gun he would not have been in such a hurry. Why not?

Clues on p. 132/Answer on p. 181

How to Choose a Builder

A man wanted to construct an important building, and he received bids from a hundred builders, who each presented their qualifications and claimed to be the best builder around. How did he eventually choose between them?

Clues on p. 133/Answer on p. 181

The Unlucky Gambler

A very unlucky gambler had lost all his money. His friends organized a raffle, rigged so that he would be sure to win. Knowing the ticket number he held, they filled a hat with tickets bearing the same number. They then had him draw the winning number. "Well," they asked him, "who won?"

"Not me, anyway," he replied sadly. What had happened?

Clues on p. 133/Answer on p. 182

Brush-off

Amanda was doing something important when she received a phone call from Zoe, who was long-winded and boring. How did Amanda quickly finish the call without offending Zoe?

Clues on p. 133/Answer on p. 182

The Code

The doorman at an exclusive club says one word to each prospective entrant. If the entrant answers correctly he is allowed to enter; otherwise, he is rejected.

A hopeful non-member observed carefully as a member approached. The doorman said, "Twelve." The member replied, "Six." He was admitted. A second member came up. The doorman said, "Six." The member replied, "Three." He was admitted. The man now decided that this was easy, and he stepped forward. The doorman said, "Ten." The man replied, "Five." The doorman angrily kicked him out. What should he have said?

Clues on p. 134/Answer on p. 182

Time of Arrival

A teenage boy returned home from a party very late and silently crept upstairs to his bedroom. No one saw or heard him arrive. The next morning when his mother asked him what time he got home, he replied, "About one o'clock." How did she know that he had, in fact, arrived much later?

Clues on p. 134/Answer on p. 182

Depressurization

A pilot was flying alone at 30,000 feet altitude when he heard a rattling noise in the plane. He immediately depressurized the plane, i.e., let the air out and allowed the pressure in the plane to drop to that of the outside atmosphere. A sudden depressurization is generally considered very dangerous, so why did he do this?

Clues on p. 134/Answer on p. 182

A Solution of Paint

A problem which had caused the loss of many thousands of lives and the loss of millions of dollars worth of property was solved with a can of paint and a brush. What was the problem?

Clues on p. 134/Answer on p. 183

Strange Reactions

John and Joan, who both enjoyed their work, were given surprises one morning. John was told that he was being laid off that week because there was no further work for him. Joan was told that she was being promoted and would get a pay raise. Joan cried for the rest of the day, while John laughed. Why?

Clues on p. 135/Answer on p. 183

Striking the Elephant

A man uses a stick to strike a part of an elephant and after a few seconds it disappears. The man is then a lot richer. Why?

Clues on p. 135/Answer on p. 183

Gaze Away

A man walked into a room full of normal people. None of them would look him in the eye. Why not?

Clues on p. 135/Answer on p. 183

Desert

A man walked alone for days across a desert. He did not take water or any kind of drink with him. He did not find water. How did he survive?

Clues on p. 135/Answer on p. 183

The Deadly Diamonds

A Bedouin prince had three diamonds which he kept in a box with a sliding lid that he kept firmly closed. The box also contained two deadly cobras which would attack any stranger foolish enough to open the box. One day a thief sneaked into the prince's tent and within moments had safely stolen the diamonds. How did he do it?

Clues on p. 135/Answer on p. 184

The Archaeologist

A professor of archaeology was on an excavation at a site when he found an ancient and interesting item. He took it home and put it in his study. His wife and children were away so there was no other person in the house. He locked up and went to bed. In the morning, he was horrified to find the item gone. A thorough search showed it was not in the house. There had been no break-in, and no one else had entered or left the house. What had happened?

Clues on p. 136/Answer on p. 184

The Container

King Arthur gave one of the knights of the Round Table a bottomless metal container in which for many years he kept flesh and blood. What was it?

Clues on p. 136/Answer on p. 184

Mutilation

Why did a man deliberately douse himself with sulfuric acid?

Clues on p. 136/Answer on p. 184

Cowardly Act

Why did a coward deliberately expose himself to significant danger?

Clues on p. 136/Answer on p. 184

Fall of the Hall

A well-designed and structurally sound building owned by the government suddenly collapsed. Why did this happen?

Clues on p. 136/Answer on p. 185

The Cicada

There is one kind of cicada (an insect sometimes known as a cricket) which has a 17-year life cycle. It lives dormant, underground, for 16 years as a grub, then emerges for one year as an active insect. What possible survival advantage can such a 17-year life cycle have?

Clues on p. 137/Answer on p. 185

Candy in Pocket

Because he had a piece of candy in his pocket, a man invented something which is found in most modern kitchens. What is it?

Clues on p. 137/Answer on p. 185

Stringing Along

A man carefully glued tiny pieces of glass to a length of string. At first he was very pleased with the results. But later he regretted doing it. Why?

Clues on p. 137/Answer on p. 186

The Painting

A painter gave his aunt an ugly abstract painting which she stored in the attic. However, when he came to stay she hurriedly hung it on the wall of her parlor. Unfortunately, she hung it upside-down. What did she say when he pointed this out?

Clues on p. 137/Answer on p. 186

Mickey Mouse's Girlfriend

Why were a group of grown men running around asking each other, "Who is Mickey Mouse's girlfriend?"

Clues on p. 137/Answer on p. 186

The Parcel

Why did a lady deliberately leave a parcel behind her on a bus?

Clues on p. 138/Answer on p. 186

The Suitcase and the Box

A man came out of a large building carrying a suitcase and box. He was very happy. He went into a smaller building and a few minutes later emerged from the smaller building very angry and carrying just the suitcase. What was going on?

Clues on p. 138/Answer on p. 187

Third Place

A man enters a competition confidently expecting to win, but he only comes in third. However, he is very amused. Why?

Clues on p. 138/Answer on p. 187

The Missing Diamond

A man kept a precious diamond in a safe. Nobody else knew the combination. It was not written down. Nobody ever saw him open the safe. Yet one day when he opened the safe, the diamond was gone. How come?

Clues on p. 138/Answer on p. 187

Paddle Your Own Canoe

A man set out to paddle his canoe down a slowly flowing river from one point to another. He found that no matter how quickly he paddled, it made no difference to the time it took for his journey. Why not?

Clues on p. 139/Answer on p. 188

Poor Impersonation

An actress is hired to impersonate an heiress who has died. The actress looks very much like the heiress. Her acting is superb. She watches videos of the woman and works tirelessly in front of a mirror to develop an excellent imitation of the woman's appearance, mannerisms, and voice. Yet she is soon exposed as an impostor. Why?

Clues on p. 139/Answer on p. 188

Doctor's Appointment

A woman has an appointment to visit the doctor. When she gets there the receptionist tells her that there is a new doctor, and that he cannot see the woman just yet as he is on the telephone. The woman waits, and then the doctor calls her in and says that he is sorry he kept her waiting, but he had some important telephone calls to handle. Within moments the doctor is highly embarrassed. Why?

Clues on p. 139/Answer on p. 188

Creepy Crawlies

A man moves into a new house and finds that his garden is crawling with insects, slugs, snails, caterpillars, and unwanted bugs. He goes to his local cinema, community hall, and bars (where he knows nobody) and asks for a donation to help clear his garden. Everyone responds very generously, and he is able to solve his problem. What happened?

Clues on p. 139/Answer on p. 188

Sweet Wheat

A farmer wins first prize for his wheat every year in an agricultural show against his neighboring farmers. However, after the show is over, he sends each of his fellow competitors a bag of his best wheat seed. Why?

Clues on p. 140/Answer on p. 189

Three Notes

One morning a woman wrote the same note to three different people. The first was a bank robber, who laughed at the note and threw it away. The second was a Bolivian, who also threw the note away. The third was a priest, who was very sad to receive the note. What was happening?

Clues on p. 140/Answer on p. 189

Catching a Bullet

A man fires a bullet from a gun and another man catches it with his bare hands. The bullet does not touch anything (except air, of course) from the gun to the hand. The second man is uninjured. How does he do it? (There are two good solutions. Can you find them both?)

Clues on p. 140/Answers on p. 189

The Clues

The Late Report

- The man was not involved in any way in the death of the person whose body he had reported.

- The man had not noticed the body earlier, but did later.

The Stranger in the Bar

- The two men were drinking beer, while the stranger was drinking soda water.

- The two men hadn't noticed the stranger outside the bars, but there was a connection between them and the stranger.

Gertrude

- Gertrude caused a mechanical failure in the plane.

- It was a jet aircraft.

Mad Cow Ideas

- The Cambodian government suggested a way for Britain to get rid of the suspect cattle without risking that the cattle would eventually be eaten.

- The suggestion involved the eventual death of the cattle in a way that would help solve a Cambodian problem.

February 1866

- It was clearly visible to man but not of man's doing.
- February 1866 lacked something that other months have.

The Cabbie's Revenge

- The cabbie did not insult the American. He did not make any personal or nationalistic comment.
- The cabbie gave the American a piece of factual information which the American did not want to hear. (We cannot tell you exactly what the cabbie said because it might ruin an evening for you, too!)
- The location to which the American was driven by the cabbie is important.

Where in the World?

- Their images are found together in one common place.
- They are found on something which is in common use and has been for many years.
- They are used in a form of game.

Scout's Honor

- She sent him to the inspection with the marks still on his hands.
- She ensured that the marks would not be seen.

The King's Favor

- In a way, the King got what he wanted, and the College got what it wanted.
- The King took the portrait along with him when he left Cambridge.
- No copy was made.

Price Tag

- A price set at 5 cents, or even 1 cent, under a round dollar amount means that a customer would be entitled to change from a bill.
- Smart shopkeepers were trying to protect themselves from losses.

Color-Blind

- He was employed by the military.
- He could see things other people found difficult to see.

Seaside Idea

- He was a senior officer in the Royal Air Force.

- He and his children threw stones into the sea.

The Hammer

- Adam did not use the hammer on the computer. The computer was undamaged.

- Brenda had a disability.

The Stranger in the Hotel

- Hers was a single room.

- There was nothing unusual about the man's appearance or bearing. The woman made a deduction based on what he said.

Buttons

- This is not a fashion issue. It has to do with right- and left-handedness.

- When buttons first came into use, it was the better-off who used them.

Upstairs, Downstairs

- The restaurant is in an unusual location.

Inner Ear

- The mother lures the insect out of her daughter's ear.

Inspired Composition

- He saw something which made no sound but which suggested a tune.
- He saw some creatures at rest.

Early Morning in Las Vegas

- The person who banged on the door was not a hotel official, nor a police officer or other such authority.
- The gambler was not in danger.

Large Number

- The answer can be quickly and accurately deduced.
- Think about the effect of actually multiplying the number of fingers on the left hands of all the people in the world, one after another.
- The calculation might start $5 \times 5 \times 5 \times 5 \times 5 \times 5 \times 5 \times 5 \times 4 \times 5 \times 5 \times 5 \times 5 \times \ldots$ and so on.

Souper

- She was perfectly capable of consuming the soup with a spoon. There was nothing wrong with the soup.
- Something happened halfway through the course which caused her to want to use the straw.

The Single Flower

- She got some help.
- No other person was involved.

Unseen

- It is known that this man led a secluded life.
- Other men, even those blind from birth, would hear and touch this thing, but this man never heard nor touched it.

The Champion's Blind Spot

- The winner had perfect eyesight and could see as well as any other person there, but they could see something he could not see.
- He could not see something relative to him which others could see relative to them.
- If the winner had lost a game, then he could not make this claim.

The Task

- The person who is performing the task has a disability.
- Circumstances have changed so that the person's disability gives him an advantage over the others.

What a Jump!

- He was an athlete.
- He did not use any extra source of power but did use special equipment.
- This happens regularly in a certain sporting event.

The String and the Cloth

- He died an accidental death.
- He had been holding the string.
- It was a windy day.

A Riddle

- They played seriously and each did his best.
- Each man came out ahead.
- No one joined their group.

Bad Impression

- He deliberately sprayed water over the paintings. This damaged them.
- He was not unstable, deranged or malevolent. He acted out of good intentions.

The Animal

- Marmaduke was able to deduce what the animal was from Alan Quartermaine's statement alone.
- Only one animal has just four knees.

Escape

- He did not attract or receive help in the form of a boat or a plane. He crossed the lake under his own power.
- He was lucky to have found shelter.

Poisoned

- The man was trying to gain sympathy. He was deceived.
- The man wrote a suicide note and then deliberately took an overdose.
- He did not intend to die. He expected to be rescued.

Failed Forgery

- The paper he used was perfect. The color, texture, and watermark were perfect.
- His copy was accurate in every way, yet the bills he made had an error that made them easily identifiable as forgeries.

Apprehended

- The burglar left no clues inside the house.
- The incident took place in the middle of winter.

The Metal Ball

- The magician need not do anything to make the ball vanish.
- He carefully makes and stores the ball before his act.

One Croaked!

- The frogs were physically identical. One managed to survive the ordeal because of the result of its actions.
- The nature of the liquid is important.

Unspoken Understanding

- The man did want two tokens, and the cashier was able to correctly deduce this.
- Nothing was written or signaled.

His Widow's Sister

- When Jim Jones died, his wife became a widow.

- No bigamy or life-after-death is involved.

- He had married his widow's sister quite legitimately.

Light Years Ahead

- There is a way in which we can see the light which we radiated and, therefore, an image of the way we were.

- It is a common experience to view this image.

The Newspaper

- Jim and Joe were normal boys aged seven and eight.

- They both stood on the same sheet of newspaper but, try as they might, they could not touch or even see each other without leaving the newspaper.

Light Work

- With just two bulbs and two switches, it would be easy.

- Light bulbs give out light. What else do they do when they are switched on?

What a Bore!

- The woman arranges an interruption, but no one else is involved.

- She enjoys the advantages of modern technology.

Soviet Pictures

- A fault was found in the photograph which proved it had been tampered with.

- A fault was discovered by a Count.

Penniless

- The author did not know the identity of the lady admirer.
- His wife was not jealous or concerned about the gift.

The Deadly Suitcase

- The body was that of a child who had died accidentally through suffocation.
- The woman was poor and had tried to save money.

Unknown Character

- He called someone who did not know him.
- By calling this person he hoped to prove that he was not a bad character.

Gasoline Problem

- No complex mathematical combinations are needed to solve this one.

Poison Pen

- They examined the letter very carefully.
- The letter came from a pad of writing paper.

The Coconut Millionaire

- He lost money on every coconut he sold.
- He did not make money by any related activity.

The Music Stopped Again

- This has nothing to do with tightrope walkers!
- A game was taking place. It involved music.

Disreputable

- This is really three puzzles in one.
- He was born after his father was. He did not murder his mother. He did not commit incest.

Personality Plus

- The client submitted handwriting tests. He then simply showed that the assessments were incorrect.

Gambler's Ruin

- They played cards, but Joe chose a game that suited him better than it suited Syd.
- Syd had a handicap at this particular child's game.

Fast Work

- Marion had committed no crime.
- She was single.

The Flicker

- He knew that someone had died.
- The piece of paper could have saved a life.

An American Shooting

- Although an innocent man was killed, no crime was committed.
- Both men were armed.
- This took place in the 19th century.

King George

- It was decided that the title might mislead audiences.

Fallen Angel

- The butterfly was not a live butterfly.
- The man walked into trouble.
- The model butterfly served as a warning.

The Flaw in the Carpet

- The shop explained that, although there was a flaw in the carpet, it was not the result of an error or mistake.
- The carpet makers were devout Muslims.

What a Relief!

- The soldier's urine contained something of use to the doctor.
- The soldier was an American GI.
- This was a common practice among many French doctors.

First Choice

- This had nothing to do with taste, nutrition, diet, or food.
- There was a practical reason why rich ladies preferred soup in restaurants. It did not apply at home.

Disturbance

- He was trying to warn them.
- They were not in danger, but he thought they were.

Mona Lisa

- They did it for money.
- No insurance payment was involved. The thieves did not receive any reward or payment from the police, museum, insurance company, or any public body.

Snow Joy

- Naturally, the children would much rather be at home, or out playing, than go to school.
- There was nothing special going on at school to attract the children back.
- There was a consequence of an extended school cancellation which they did not want.

The Cheat

- The man had failed to keep a promise.
- He had not used the $5 as agreed.
- The woman found herself considerably worse off than she had expected.

Dutch Race

- The race can only take place under certain conditions. These conditions occur infrequently.

Wino

- He did not want to eat the dessert, but didn't want to appear rude.
- He was hungry, normally enjoyed this dessert and had started it with gusto. It had tasted good, and he felt fine.

Garden Story

- The man had lied, but not with the intention of deceiving his wife.

- He was worried that the hard work of gardening would be a strain for his wife, who lived alone and had no one to help her.

Fireworks Display

- The family consisted of two parents, their four-year-old daughter and their two-month-old baby son.

- The fireworks display went perfectly. There were no accidents or injuries. The children enjoyed it.

- The parents learned something.

The Fallen Guide

- The first guide fell into the deep ravine and was lost from view. Both the climber and the second guide were fit and healthy. They had time to try to rescue the first guide, but they did not bother.

- The climber believed that the first guide was not important to him and could be replaced.

The Yacht Incident

- They had been passengers aboard the yacht.

- They died because of an accident. They drowned.

Self-Addressed Envelope

- He posts a letter so that he will receive a letter.
- He wants to be sure of seeing the postman on every possible delivery.

Fingered

- He was vain.
- He wanted maximum publicity.

The Gross Grocery List

- The grocery list contained nothing more than a list of regular and ordinary groceries.
- The man to whom she handed the list was not a grocer.
- She had set out that morning with two lists.

Finger Break

- She had good intentions.
- He was in danger.

Unpublished

- The publication of the novel would not cause offense or any legal actions.
- The title of the novel was well-known.

The Unwanted Gift

- The gift was costly to maintain.
- The gift was of a rare color.

Benjamin Franklin

- Benjamin Franklin deliberately spelled Philadelphia wrongly as part of his job. He was not involved in teaching.
- He was trying to make things more difficult for those who made his job difficult.

Middle Eastern Muddle

- They produced an ad which was misunderstood.
- Their ad had no words.

The Wounded Soldier

- The soldier was genuinely wounded and was not a coward. The doctor knew this.
- The doctor lied, but had good intentions and wanted to help the soldier.

Ice Rinked

- She misunderstood his intentions.
- Although he did not say a word, he did try to communicate with her.

On Time

- He was not interested in the time.
- He wanted to make an innocuous telephone call.
- He was cheating.

Cat Food

- He wanted the cat to do something for him.

Rich Man, Poor Man

- The man makes over $10 million a year at his work but he does not have a lot to spend.
- He is not wealthy and doesn't have any major debts or expenses.

Sleeping on the Job

- The man was a movie star.
- The people who lost their jobs worked in the garment industry.

Fine Art

- The art collector learned that his two very valuable works were worth far less than he had assumed.
- There was no mistake. Sotheby's correctly identified the works.

Ford's Lunch

- Henry Ford was giving the person a form of test, although the candidate for the position did not realize it.
- He watched carefully as the candidate consumed his soup.

The Hairdresser

- The New York hairdresser had nothing against New Yorkers and has no particular love of Canadians.
- He charges everyone the same price for one haircut.

Not a Hair

- Everyone else who was caught in the rain was soaked.
- Lyndsey's head got wet.

The Plate of Mushrooms

- Although he still believed that one or more of the mushrooms might be poisonous, he no longer feared that the mushrooms would kill him.

Order Delayed

- The drink he ordered is relevant.
- It was a type of soda.

Silence Is Golden

- The audience was not physically restrained from applauding the speaker. They simply chose not to.

- The audience was made up entirely of women.

Bluebeard's Treasure

- The map did show the exact location of the treasure and the enemy would be able to reach the island and excavate the spot.

- Bluebeard buried treasure in a way which he believed optimized his chances of recovering it.

The King

- Twelve men had started out in the attempt to become king. The one who succeeded was one of the few to survive.

Lockout

- Given enough time, the burglar could pick each lock in turn, i.e., he could change its state from locked to unlocked or vice-versa.
- It took the burglar half an hour to pick a lock. After two days of picking the locks he gave up and went home.

Creepy Crawly

- It was not dangerous.
- It was not alive—nor had it ever been.

The Unlucky Trip

- The torch was important.
- The man was a runner.

Checked

- His signature was perfect.
- He intended to defraud. The check looked fine but it would not have proven valid.

Fruitless Search

- Blue-back frogs are now extinct.
- The man was very religious.
- He wanted to get back to his boat.

Truckload

- It is true that, when the starlings alight on the truck, their weight adds to it.
- Despite the birds landing on the truck, the total weight of truck and birds never exceeds 10 tons.

The Deadly Melody

- She was in her home when this happened.
- She had heard the tune many times before. Normally she was happy when she heard this tune.
- The stranger was trying to rob her.

The Sign

- The sign was inside the car and the car was stationary.
- He shot her because he learned she had been having an affair.

New Shoes

- She died because she wore the new shoes.
- She was involved in entertainment.

The Archduke

- He was very vain.
- His coat had no buttons or zippers.

The Hasty Packer

- She packed one essential item for a particular kind of journey.
- She packed material and string.

Heartless

- The man's profession is important.

Dead Drunk

- He died an accidental death as a result of his actions and where he was.

- He was alone at a subway station.

The Big Room

- He died because he went back for the brandy.

- He drowned.

Sacrifice

- They did not choose by chance but agreed between them based on a good reason, which even the one chosen had to admit was sound.

- They had different beliefs and philosophies.

Stolen Finger

- He wanted to send it to someone.

- He wanted someone to think it was his finger.

Poor Dogs

- They had trained the dogs with the intention of inflicting harm on enemies.
- The dogs did exactly what they had been trained to do.

Radio Death

- He had been expecting to hear the piece of music that he heard, but had not planned to commit suicide.
- There was something about the way the music was playing which meant that he was in very serious trouble.

Thirsty

- The man was fit and not hampered in his movements.
- There was plenty of water in and near his home.

Aftershave

- He died an accidental death.
- He died because his smell was different.

Capsize

- It overbalanced when the weight distribution on the boat suddenly changed.
- Something quite light dropped onto one side of the boat.

Untying the Ropes

- Ropes were not involved in the way the man died, nor was he tied up in the ropes.

- Untying the ropes was a form of signal.

Murder in the Newspaper

- His profession is important.

- He had met the murderer.

The Man Who Returned Too Soon

- He died an accidental death. No other person or creature was involved.

- The danger was not in his home. What killed him was the fact that he returned too quickly.

The Truck Driver

- He was killed accidentally. No other person or creature was involved.

- He had sensed that something was wrong with his truck. He was right. His death and the problem with the truck were linked.

The Circle and the Line

- They died an accidental death in the course of a journey.

- They could see the line drawing nearer. However, the line never moved.

The Perfect Murder

- He had caused something to fall so that its motion would be detected by the burglar alarm sensors.

- No electrical, telephone, or radio devices were used. He did not use any spring or complex mechanical device. He used something much simpler.

The Sniper

- The sniper is determined to shoot him and will come to the car to do so if he takes cover.

- Attack is the best form of defense.

Fair Deal

- There was nothing faked or pretended about this incident. The dealer had murdered the man who was stabbed.
- The dealer was punished for the crime.

The Cloth

- The man who waved the cloth knew that his action would probably cause a man to die.
- He did not know which man would die.
- The man died of a gunshot.

Bostonian

- There was nothing strange or unusual about this man.
- His friends and neighbors in Boston were also not U.S. citizens.

The Tree and the Axe

- She used the axe to destroy the tree that she had recently bought.
- She did not buy the tree in order to put it into the garden.

Below Par

- He was not pleased because it was not a good score.

School Friend

- Joe did not know who had married his friend. He had no other source of information than this conversation.
- He knew that the girl's mother was called Louise.

Sell More Beer

- The consultant gave the bar owner a piece of advice that many of the bar's customers would have been glad to hear.
- Implementing the advice would benefit the customers more than the bar owner.

The Lumberjacks

- During his breaks, Joe does something which helps him to cut more trees.

The Clinch

- Something caused them to be locked together even though they wanted to part.

Precognition

- The profession of the lady who knocked at the door is important.

Dud Car

- The Nova had a poor image, even though it was a good automobile.
- People laughed when they heard of it.

Red Light

- The police officer was perfectly capable of chasing the teenagers, and he was not engaged in any other task at the time.
- The officer was conscientious and always chased and apprehended those he saw breaking the law.

Nun-plussed

- The doctor smiled and explained that he had cured the nun's complaint.

Confectionery Manufacturer

- The confectionery is a popular and healthy food.
- The workers are always very busy.

The Painter

- He was a very good painter whose work could be seen at art galleries and private houses.
- He was not shy of publicity and he used his own name.
- He did not paint on canvas.

Regular Arguments

- It was the same topic and conversation which led them to quarrel every night.
- On Saturdays they argued in the afternoon as well.

Beautiful Girls

- He paid in order to get a beautiful girl on each arm.

Orange Trick

- The second orange goes under the first orange, but the first orange remains on the table.

The Fall

- The man had no special skills or training. Many other people can do this.
- Some people find this kind of fall enjoyable. Others are terrified.

The Bookmark

- He has what he considers a better alternative.

Good-bye, Mother

- The old lady had a mean purpose in mind when she asked the young woman the favor.

Steer Clear of the Banks

- Roller-blading, cycling and running were all forbidden on the road.

A Hairy Story

- No wigs, potions, or transplants were involved.

- After her actions, his hair looked exactly like hers.

By the River

- The man had intended to fire the gun.

- No one was in danger.

- He would not have used the gun if he had not been near the river.

The Helicopter

- It was a real helicopter hovering over a real sea. The helicopter stopped flying and stopped hovering, but it did not hit the sea.
- The helicopter was owned by an oil company.

Car in the River

- He did not have any special equipment or powers.
- He breathed normally throughout the whole incident.

Pay Phone

- She gave the telephone company a strong incentive to fix the pay phone.
- She told the telephone company that some people were very pleased that the telephone did not work properly.

The Typist

- She was chosen on merit.
- She was a good typist.

Two Jugs

- There was no divider in the vat; it was one large container.

- After the pourings, the vat contained all the lemonade and all the milk—yet they were separate.

- If you could have heard the operation, you would know the answer.

Speeding Ticket

- It was not a one-way street and there was nothing wrong or unusual about the car.

- He was breaking the general speed limit.

Twin Trouble

- They were normal natural twins.

- Bob was born first, but the birth certificates correctly showed Sam's time of birth before Bob's.

Library Lunacy

- The library benefited from this temporary change in the rules.

- This relaxation of the normal rules of borrowing was a one-time event caused by something else which was happening at the library.

Elevator

- She was not alone in the elevator.
- There was a misunderstanding.

Fall of the Wall

- The construction of the wall was sound. It did not have any structural or mechanical weaknesses.
- The wall was breached through subtlety rather than through force.

Smart Appearance

- Professional help had been involved in making Victor look particularly smart.
- Everyone noticed how smart he looked but no one spoke to him.

Dogs Home

- The truck had two doors at the back.
- One door was open and one was closed.

Title Role

- She had been given the role of a beautiful and successful woman.
- The book is by Daphne du Maurier. It concerns a woman who dies under mysterious circumstances.

Job Lot

- They had been designed for a specific purpose.
- They would be very useful for one type of building.

The Lifeboat

- He was not rescued during the two days, nor did he see land or any other refuge.
- The lifeboat was old-fashioned in design and construction.

Invaluable

- The man was a criminal.
- He was both lucky and unlucky.

The Crash

- The police were not surprised that they could not find any drivers for the cars.
- No one had left the scene of the accident.

Westward Ho!

- They walked only in an eastward direction. They never reached or passed through London.
- The location of the restaurant is important.

40 Feet Ahead

- He was a normal man who walked in a normal fashion.

- It was a long walk.

The Circular Table

- She solved the problem easily and without special equipment.

- She used a piece of paper.

T-Shirts

- The T-shirts were designed to circumvent the law.
- The law was a traffic regulation.
- The black band was a diagonal stripe.

Two Suitcases

- He does not intend to carry the suitcase far.
- He is trying to save money.

The Nonchalant Police Officer

- He was not cowardly nor neglecting his duty.
- No one else in the street took any notice of the robbers, even though they were seen by several passers-by.

Rare Event

- This is not an astronomical, geological, or physical event.
- The answer relates to the date. The last time it happened was in the days of the Beatles and John F. Kennedy.

Holy Orders

- The priest was a real priest carrying a real gun. He was not a criminal, and no crime was involved.
- He wanted to shoot something.
- The gun was used to solve an unsightly problem.

Well-Dressed

- She was not cold and did not need to wear her hat and coat.
- She did it for her convenience and to avoid a difficult situation.
- She liked to chat but only to her friends.

Kid Stuff

- The expert's theory has nothing to do with the behavior of children.
- It has to do with the appearance of children to the motorist.

The Two Drivers

- Although the two drivers had driven in identical fashion, one had committed an offense and the other had not. The police officer acted properly.
- It happened in a hot country.

Keys in the Car

- The man did not mean to lock his keys in the car. He had no criminal or ulterior motive. It was an accident.

- When he had been unable to retrieve his keys, the man had initiated another course of action in order to get them.

The Hasty Robber

- The other gun was not in the bank.

- He was apprehended by the police, but not for robbery.

How to Choose a Builder

- He had no knowledge of building or of the builders' experience.

- He did not decide on price. He wanted a reliable builder of good reputation and quality.

- He enlisted the help of the builders in selecting one who met his requirements.

The Unlucky Gambler

- What he had drawn from the hat did not bear the number 77, yet the only things that his friends had put in the hat were tickets with the number 77.

Brush-off

- Amanda did not invent any excuse or pretense.

- She wanted Zoe to think that they had been accidentally interrupted.

The Code

- The members and the doorman were consistent and logical in what they said and did. There was a code based solely on the numbers, which they followed.

- The code would work in other languages but probably with different combinations of numbers. (For example, in Italian the doorman might say "Otto" and the member reply, "Quattro.")

Time of Arrival

- The mother deduced correctly from what she saw that he must have come home very late.

- When he came in, the boy did not make a sound. He removed his boots and then crept up to bed.

Depressurization

- He did this for his own safety.

- The rattle alerted him to a problem which might become dangerous.

A Solution of Paint

- The problem concerned transportation. The use of the paint stopped overloading.

Strange Reactions

- Joan was pleased at the news of her promotion. John was disappointed to learn that he was losing his job.
- The nature of their work is important.

Striking the Elephant

- The man is very skillful in his use of the stick.
- The man strikes something made of ivory.

Gaze Away

- The man was physically normal, yet he was different from all the other people.
- Everyone treated him with great respect.

Desert

- People need to have water in their bodies in order to survive. How did the man get it?
- No other person or creature is involved.
- He did not find liquids of any kind in the desert.

The Deadly Diamonds

- The thief did not use any special powers or materials to subdue or control the snakes.
- The thief opened the box in a way which allowed him to safely extract the diamonds.

The Archaeologist

- The item had been removed from the house.
- When his wife was away, the archaeologist went for a walk every morning and evening. When she was at home, they took turns going for walks.

The Container

- It was a common article then and now.

Mutilation

- The man was a criminal.
- He hoped to escape detection.

Cowardly Act

- He risked pain and physical injury because he thought that he might thereby avoid a greater risk.
- He hoped to get shot.

Fall of the Hall

- No animal activity or change in the state of the building components or structure is involved.
- It had been used for a different purpose than that for which it was designed.

The Cicada

- It is thought that the 17-year life cycle of the cicada gives it additional protection against predators. But it is not safer underground than any other such grub, nor safer as an insect than any other cicada.

Candy in Pocket

- The man noticed that the candy in his pocket was affected by something with which he was experimenting.
- The invention is used in cooking.

Stringing Along

- He used the string in a competition.
- He gained an unfair advantage over his rivals.

The Painting

- She tried not to hurt his feelings.
- She claimed to like and understand the painting.

Mickey Mouse's Girlfriend

- It was a deadly serious exercise.
- It was a test.

The Parcel

- It was something that she made for someone else.
- She knew it would probably be found and handed in.

The Suitcase and the Box

- He had gained his freedom but lost something dear to him.
- The suitcase and the box had contained the personal belongings he had had for several years.
- The smaller building was a bar into which he had gone to celebrate and to show off the contents of the box.

Third Place

- It was an acting contest.
- The man was a famous actor and movie star.
- The contest was for fun.

The Missing Diamond

- An enterprising thief had worked out a way of figuring out the combination.
- The thief had left something in the room.

Paddle Your Own Canoe

- The man and the canoe were normal, but the river was unusual.
- He could do this only at a certain time of year.

Poor Impersonation

- The actress was found out because she had used a mirror to rehearse.
- Her voice was faultless. She looked exactly like the heiress in all regards except one.

Doctor's Appointment

- The doctor and the woman had never met and there was no prior connection between them.
- The doctor was embarrassed when he found out why the woman was there.
- The doctor was trying to create a good impression on his first day.

Creepy Crawlies

- He poisoned the bugs.
- The places he went gave him what was worthless to them but useful to him.

Sweet Wheat

- His primary concern is to ensure that his wheat will be of the finest quality.

- He is quite happy for his neighbors to grow his strain of wheat and thereby produce better wheat. He gains by this.

Three Notes

- She had never met any of the three people and had no intention of meeting them, but her note was a serious communication.

- The bank robber was part of a gang and had a specific role in the planned robbery.

- The Bolivian was a tourist.

Catching a Bullet

- The second man had no special powers or protection. However, in each solution he would need very precise positioning.

- The bullet is a normal bullet fired from a normal gun and is normally deadly.

- When the man catches the bullet, it is travelling slowly.

The Answers

The Late Report

The man saw the body in the background on one of his holiday photographs. It was two months before the film was developed.

The Stranger in the Bar

He said, "I am the taxi driver who has been driving you from bar to bar!"

Gertrude

Gertrude, a goose, had been sucked into a jet engine.

Mad Cow Ideas

The Cambodian Government suggested that the cattle be sent to Cambodia and allowed to wander their fields to blow up the many mines left over from their wars.

February 1866

There was no full moon. January and March of that year each had two full moons—a most unusual occurrence.

The Cabbie's Revenge

The American was going to a performance of the famous Agatha Christie play "The Mousetrap." The taxi dropped him outside the theater. The spiteful taxi driver said "X did it," where X was the name of the murderer in the play. (We cannot state X's name or we might ruin your future enjoyment of the play!)

Where in the World?

On a pack of playing cards. The original designs for the Kings, Queens, and Jacks are based on these characters.

Scout's Honor

She covered the stains with a Band-Aid. Nobody would remove it to check whether he had a cut.

The King's Favor

The College asked the King to return the painting in six months. Since this was clearly in his power, he agreed.

Price Tag

The practice originated to ensure that the clerk had to open the till and give change for each transaction, thus recording the sale and preventing him from pocketing the bills.

Color-Blind

John was employed by the Air Force during wartime to detect camouflaged enemy positions from aerial photographs. Camouflage is designed to fool people with normal vision. People who are color-blind are much better at spotting differences in the texture and shading of landscape.

Seaside Idea

As he watched his children skimming stones on the water he got the idea for the famous bouncing bombs used by the "Dam Busters" in their raid against German dams. The bombs bounced along the surface of the lakes before hitting the dams and flooding large industrial areas.

The Hammer

Brenda was blind and she depended on her Braille manual when using the computer. Alan flattened the pages with a hammer.

The Stranger in the Hotel

She reasoned that if it had really been his room he would not have knocked at the door but used his key. (She was on a corridor of single rooms, so it was unlikely he was sharing.) In fact, he knocked in order to check whether anyone was in before using a pass key to enter and burgle rooms.

Buttons

Most people are right-handed and find it easier to fasten a button which is on the right through a hole which is on the left. This is why men's buttons are on the right. When buttons were first used it was the better-off who could afford clothes with buttons. Among this class the ladies were often dressed by maid-servants. The servant would face the lady and so it was easier for right-handed servants to fasten buttons which were on the lady's left.

Upstairs, Downstairs

It is the First Class restaurant on a luxury ocean liner. Upstairs is out on deck. If it rains, the entire company transfers downstairs and takes up where it left off.

Inner Ear

She put the girl in a darkened room and placed a bright light near her ear. The insect emerged.

Inspired Composition

He saw some blackbirds sitting on telegraph wires. Their positions indicated a melody line.

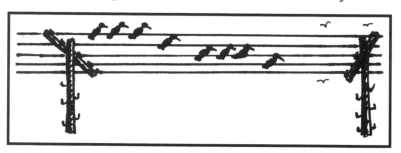

Early Morning in Las Vegas

He had played poker in his room with friends until 2 a.m. They had all had plenty to drink, and he had failed to notice that one of his friends had fallen asleep behind his sofa. Later, the man woke up and rattled the door as he tried to get out. The gambler let him out.

Large Number

The product of the number of fingers on the left hands of every person is zero. It only takes one person to have no fingers on their left hand for the product to be zero, because anything multiplied by zero is zero.

Souper

Her contact lens had fallen into the soup, and she wanted to retrieve it.

The Single Flower

She opened the window and a bee flew into the room. It settled on the one true flower.

Unseen

A woman! The man was Mihailo Tolotos, who was taken from his mother at birth and who spent all his life in the Greek monastery of Athos, where no females were allowed.

The Champion's Blind Spot

Every other competitor could see someone who had beaten them.

The Task

This is a true story that happened years ago in New York during a power outage. A telephone exchange in a large apartment building was working on an independent power supply. Many people wanted to phone out, to reassure friends and relatives. They were helped in this by a blind man, who could do a much better job of dialing numbers in the darkness than any of them could.

What a Jump!

It was a ski jump.

The String and the Cloth

His kite had snagged on some power lines. It was raining. He had been electrocuted. The cloth and string were the remains of the kite.

A Riddle

For the music they played,
Each band member was paid.

Bad Impression

He was a firefighter who, in the course of putting out a fire, sprayed the room and paintings with water. He had indeed damaged the paintings, but saved them and others from complete destruction.

The Animal

Marmaduke knew that the only animal with four knees is the elephant.

Escape

He walked over the frozen lake.

Poisoned

The man was separated from his wife but wanted to be reconciled. His nephew, and heir, suggested showing how distraught he was at the loss of his wife by staging a suicide attempt and taking an overdose. The nephew agreed to take the man's farewell letter to his wife so that she would rush over and save the man. Instead of doing so, the callous nephew stuck a stamp on it and posted it. By the time the wife reached her husband, he was dead.

Failed Forgery

He had copied a forged bill which itself contained a flaw.

Apprehended

It was during winter and the place was covered in snow. As the burglar backed his car to leave, he hit a snowbank and his license plate left a perfect impression in the snow.

The Metal Ball

The disappearing ball was a ball of frozen mercury, which was taken from a freezer. It melted during the course of the act.

One Croaked!

The frogs fell into a large tank of cream. One swam around for a while but then gave up and drowned. The other kept swimming until his movements turned the cream into knobs of butter, on which he safely floated.

Unspoken Understanding

He gives the cashier four quarters, from which the cashier correctly deduces that the man wants two 40-cent tokens.

His Widow's Sister

Jim Jones married Ella in 1820. She died in 1830. In 1840 he married Ella's sister, Mary. She became his widow when he died in 1850. So in 1820 he had married his widow's sister.

Light Years Ahead

Yes—if you look in a mirror then you see light which left your body a finite time ago and has been reflected to reach your eyes. You see yourself as you were—not as you are!

The Newspaper

She slid the sheet of newspaper under a door. The boys stood on either side of the door but on the same piece of paper.

Light Work

You set switches A and B on and switch C off. You wait a few minutes and then switch B off. You then enter the room. The bulb which is on is connected to A. The cold bulb which is off is connected to C. The warm bulb which is off is connected to B.

What a Bore!

She has a cellular phone in her pocket. Discreetly, she presses a button on it that causes it to give a test ring. She pretends that she has been awaiting an important call that she must take.

Soviet Pictures

In a group of ten Soviet officials photographed sitting around a table there were eleven pairs of feet underneath the table.

Penniless

The author's wife was the lady admirer. She had recently received a small legacy and did not want to offend him by offering him money directly.

The Deadly Suitcase

The body was that of the woman's son. They were flying to the U.S. to start a new life, but she did not have enough money for two airfares. She put him in a suitcase with tiny airholes. She did not know that the luggage compartment would be depressurized.

Unknown Character

He called the local sheriff, who had never heard of him. He used this as proof of his good character.

Gasoline Problem

The man uses the meter at the gas pump to measure out exactly 13 gallons. He puts 11 gallons in the large container and 2 gallons into one of the others.

Poison Pen

The sheet of paper on which the letter had been written had been taken from a writing pad. On the previous sheet, the culprit had written his address. This caused a slight impression on the sheet below. The address became visible when the policeman gently shaded the sheet with pencil.

The Coconut Millionaire

The man is a philanthropist who bought great quantities of coconuts to sell to poor people at prices they could afford. He started out as a billionaire, but lost so much money in his good works that he became a millionaire!

The Music Stopped Again

He was an insect sitting on a chair seat during a game of musical chairs.

Disreputable

He was born in the presence of his father. His mother died at the birth. He became a pastor and married his sister to her husband.

Personality Plus

The man was ambidextrous. He gave two writing samples under different names—one written with his right hand and one with his left. The agency gave him two completely different personality profiles.

Gambler's Ruin

Syd Sharp was a first-class card player but he had a bad stutter. Knowing that Syd would be unable to respond fast enough to verbally announce the turning up of matching cards that the game's rules required, Joe challenged him to a game of Snap!

Fast Work

Marion had been picked up for a ride to the church. She was a member of the clergy and had married the men to their wives. (She was often heard to say that she enjoyed "Marion" people!)

The Flicker

The man was carrying a stay of execution for a condemned man who was due to die in the electric chair. When he saw the lights flicker, he knew that he was too late.

An American Shooting

This happened during the American Civil War. The men were soldiers in the opposing armies.

King George

It was believed that many cinema-goers would mistakenly think it was the third in a series of movies, and would not go to see it because they had missed the first two. It was released as "The Madness of King George."

Fallen Angel

The butterfly was made of plastic and was put on a large plate-glass window to indicate the presence of the glass. After it fell off, a man walked into the window and was seriously injured.

The Flaw in the Carpet

Every oriental carpet has a deliberate flaw in its design pattern. Islamic carpet makers believe that to make a perfect carpet would be to challenge Allah, who alone is perfect.

What a Relief!

It was to collect penicillin, the new wonder drug. It was in very short supply, but American soldiers were given it to protect them against various diseases. The easiest way for French doctors to get hold of penicillin was to extract it from the urine of the GIs.

First Choice

There had been a spate of robberies at expensive restaurants. The robbers would burst in and take jewelry and money from the people in the restaurant. If you are eating soup, then you can quietly drop rings or other jewelry into the soup before the robbers reach your table.

Disturbance

The man had seen a stranger climb into the house through a window. Fearing for their safety, he woke his neighbors up. The "intruder" was a new lodger, who had forgotten his key. The alert man was thanked for his concern.

Mona Lisa

The thieves handed the Mona Lisa back but not before they sold a dozen fake copies to gullible art collectors, each of whom believed he was buying the original. None of the buyers could go to the police because they were guilty of buying goods they believed to be stolen. By returning the original, the thieves ensured that they would get only a light punishment if they were caught.

Snow Joy

There is a rule in that county that up to six "snow days" may be lost from the school calendar due to bad weather. If the bad weather extends past six days, then each additional day lost must be made up by the school working an extra day—which is taken from the summer vacation. The children were upset that they would now lose precious holidays in the summer.

The Cheat

For five weeks in a row, the woman gave the man a dollar to buy a lottery ticket on her behalf. Feeling that her chances were nil, he kept the money. Her numbers came up on the fifth week, winning the $10 million jackpot. She told all her friends and neighbors that she had won.

Dutch Race

The race is the famous "eleven towns race," the largest natural ice race in the world. Usually 12,000–15,000 people take part over a course on the frozen canals and lakes in Holland. However, it can only take place after a long period of very cold weather. The right circumstances occur around once every ten years. The authorities prepare (for example, by banning factories from discharging warm waste water into the canals) and then give only two or three days' notice of the start of the race.

Wino

His host had sneezed, and the guest felt that his dessert had been contaminated. He did not want to eat it, nor did he want to blame his host, so he deliberately knocked the salt into the dessert. He made it look like an accident.

Garden Story

The man was in prison. He knew that all his mail was read. He received a letter from his wife asking, "When should I plant the potatoes?" He replied, "Do not plant any potatoes. I have hidden some guns in the garden." A little later his wife wrote back, "Some policemen came and dug up all the back garden, but they did not find anything." He replied, "Now plant the potatoes."

Fireworks Display

The parents discovered that their baby son was deaf. He reacted to the sight of fireworks but not to loud bangs of fireworks which were out of sight.

The Fallen Guide

One of the guides was a book.

The Yacht Incident

All of the people on the yacht went swimming. No one put a rope ladder over the side. They were unable to get back on board again.

Self-Addressed Envelope

The man lives in a remote spot, ten miles from the bar in the nearest village. If the postman calls on him to deliver any mail, then the man can get a lift from the postman into the village. Otherwise he has to pay for a taxi. He secretly sends himself a letter every day to get the postman to call. The postman does not deliver on Sunday, so there is no need for a letter to be posted on Saturday.

Fingered

He did this in case a photograph was being taken of the incident. He reasoned that no newspaper editor would edit out the candidate from a picture but leave his finger in.

The Gross Grocery List

The man was a priest who was rather deaf. He asked people in confession to write their sins down and put them through the grill of the confessional. When he handed her back her grocery list, the woman realized that she must have given her list of sins to the grocer.

Finger Break

He was holding a live electric cable. The electricity had paralyzed the muscles in his arm. Her action freed him.

Unpublished

The manuscript was for the book of the famous play "The Mousetrap" by Agatha Christie. She had requested that for as long as it ran as a play in London's West End, it should not be published as a novel (for fear of giving away the play's secret). Little could she have foreseen that the play would set a world record for the longest run of over 40 years of continuous performances.

The Unwanted Gift

The King was the King of Siam and the gift was a white elephant. The story goes that the King gave the gift of a rare white elephant to those with whom he was displeased and wished to ruin. The elephant was very expensive to keep but was sacred and could not be used for work. Also as a royal gift, it could not be disposed of. This is the source of the expression "a white elephant."

Benjamin Franklin

Benjamin Franklin was at one time in charge of the U.S. Mint. Forgery of bank notes was a great problem. He deliberately misspelled Philadelphia on a banknote in order to enable the detection of forgeries. Unfortunately for him, the forgers simply copied his deliberate mistake.

Middle Eastern Muddle

The agency forgot that people in the Middle East read from right to left. People saw a series of pictures showing the "before" and "after" for the use of washing powder. It indicated to them that the powder made clean clothes dirty.

The Wounded Soldier

The surgeon had run out of life-saving adrenaline. He knew that the soldier was badly wounded and hoped to provoke a rush of natural adrenaline through the soldier's reaction to his false accusation.

Ice Rinked

As he approached the woman, he made a sign to ask if she was OK. He put his thumb and first finger together to make an O. This sign is often used in countries such as the U.S. or U.K. to mean, "Are you all right?" Unfortunately, the woman came from an Eastern Mediterranean country (such as Greece) where this same sign is an obscene gesture.

On Time

The man is having an affair. Once he has phoned his mistress, he calls information so that if his wife should later press the redial button, she will not find out anything he does not want her to know.

Cat Food

The man was a television cable engineer who needed to thread a cable from the back of a house, under the floor, to the front. He released the cat with a string attached to it into a hole at the back of the house. The cat was lured by the smell of the cream and salmon to find its way under the floor to the front of the house. The string was used to pull the cable through.

Rich Man, Poor Man

He works at the mint. He makes many millions of dollars a year but draws a modest salary.

Sleeping on the Job

The man was Clark Gable, the screen idol, who took off his shirt in a movie in which he was about to go to bed. He was not wearing an undershirt. So great was his influence that men stopped wearing undershirts, and factories making them had to close down. In a later movie, he wore an undershirt and restored it to fashion.

Fine Art

The collector was told that the two items were an original Stradivarius and a previously unknown work by Vincent van Gogh. Unfortunately, Stradivarius could not paint very well, and Vincent van Gogh made terrible violins!

Ford's Lunch

Henry Ford watched the potential employee eating soup. If he put salt in his soup before tasting it, then he would not employ him. Since the candidate could not know how salty the soup was without tasting it, Ford felt that this indicated a closed mind rather than someone who would investigate a situation before taking action.

The Hairdresser

He gets three times as much money!

Not a Hair

Lyndsey had accepted the role of a Deltan in a "Star Trek" movie. Deltan women are noted for shaving their heads.

The Plate of Mushrooms

He was to be executed. The mushrooms were his last meal.

Order Delayed

The man had ordered a 7-Up. The hotel receptionist had misunderstood the order for the soda to mean a wake-up call for 7 a.m.

Silence Is Golden

The talk, given by a doctor, was on the subject of breast-feeding. It was given to a group of nursing mothers all of whom had their babies with them. They agreed that applause would wake and scare the babies, so they waved their hands in the air instead.

Bluebeard's Treasure

Bluebeard buried his treasure at the spot shown on the map. He knew that a copy of the map might be made, so he dug a shaft 30 feet deep and buried three-quarters of his treasure there. He covered that and filled in the shaft to a depth of 10 feet, where he buried a quarter of his treasure—which he was prepared to sacrifice to protect the rest. He reckoned that no one who had found substantial treasure at 10 feet would dig a further 20 feet, and that once word got out that his treasure had been taken, no one else would look for it.

The King

This is normal in a game of checkers.

Lockout

Jefferson Jones left three locks locked and three locks unlocked. He knew which was in which state, but the burglar did not. When the burglar eventually picked a lock which had been unlocked, he locked it. Try as he might, he could never get all six unlocked at the same time.

Creepy Crawly

It was a coin.

The Unlucky Trip

The torch was the Olympic Torch, which the hurrying man was carrying to the opening of the Olympic Games.

Checked

He used ink which vanished after a few hours.

Fruitless Search

The man was Noah. He knew that if he did not find a second blue-back frog they would become extinct in the flood. Unfortunately, this is what happened.

Truckload

It was a long bridge, and the weight of gasoline used in reaching the center of the bridge exceeds the weight of the flock of starlings. The truck still weighs no more than 10 tons.

The Deadly Melody

The woman was alone and asleep in her house in the middle of the night when she was awakened by the sound of her musical jewel box. She knew that a burglar was in her bedroom. She reached under her pillow, pulled out a gun, and shot him.

The Sign

The car was stationary. The man's wife was deaf and dumb. She used sign language to tell her husband that she was having an affair with another man and that she was leaving him.

New Shoes

She was a knife-thrower's assistant in a circus act. He was blindfolded and threw knives at her with unerring accuracy. Unfortunately, her new shoes had much higher heels than her normal shoes. Therefore, she died.

The Archduke

Archduke Ferdinand's uniform was sewn onto him so that he looked immaculately smart. It could not be removed quickly. His desire for a perfect appearance probably cost him his life.

The Hasty Packer

She was a sky diver who packed her parachute too quickly. It did not deploy correctly when she pulled the ripcord.

Heartless

He was a mime artist giving a stage performance. When he had the heart attack, the audience thought it was all part of the act, and no one came to help him until it was too late.

Dead Drunk

He was at a deserted underground railway station. He urinated onto the electrified third rail and was electrocuted.

The Big Room

The large room is the ballroom of the Titanic. The barman went back to get a bottle of brandy for the lifeboat, but he never made it.

Sacrifice

One of the three was a strict vegetarian. He agreed that he should naturally be the sacrifice.

Stolen Finger

He had faked his own kidnapping and demanded a large ransom. He sent in someone else's finger with his ring on it to add force to the ransom demand.

Poor Dogs

During World War II, German soldiers trained dogs to carry explosive charges under tanks and then wait there until the charge exploded, destroying dog and tank. They then released the dogs near Russian tank positions. Unfortunately for the Germans, Russian tanks did not smell at all like the German tanks on which the dogs had been trained, so the dogs hunted around until they found German tanks to sit under. Consequently, they had to be shot and the whole sorry scheme abandoned.

Radio Death

The man is a disc jockey who put on a long piece of music during his show and slipped out of the studio in order to kill his wife. He had timed the plan perfectly and would claim that he was on the air throughout the evening as his alibi. After killing the woman, he drove hurriedly back and turned on the radio. He heard the music repeating as the record skipped. He knew that his cover was blown, and he shot himself.

Thirsty

His home was his ocean-going yacht. He lost his way and his radio following a storm on an ocean voyage and eventually ran out of fresh water.

Aftershave

The man was a beekeeper. The aftershave changed his smell, and the swarm of bees that knew him well now attacked him as a stranger.

Capsize

The riverboat was crowded with passengers and was motoring down a tropical river when a large snake fell off an overhanging branch onto the boat. All the passengers rushed to the other side of the boat to get away from the snake. This unbalanced the boat, which capsized.

Untying the Ropes

When the president was shot, he was rushed to the hospital in serious condition. When he died, all the ropes on the flagpoles across the country were loosened, as the flags were flown at half-mast.

Murder in the Newspaper

The old man was a priest, and he was sitting alone when he read the newspaper. That day a man had confessed to him that he had murdered his aunt for her money. The priest realized that the woman in the newspaper was the murder victim. The seal of the confessional meant that he could not report the incident to the police.

The Man Who Returned Too Soon

His home was a houseboat on the sea. He put on his scuba gear and dived 200 feet. One should ascend from such a depth slowly in order to depressurize. He came up too quickly and suffered a severe attack of the "bends," from which he died.

The Truck Driver

One of the wheels of the truck had worked loose and come off a little earlier. It had continued to roll along the road. As he stood by his truck, he was hit by the runaway wheel.

The Circle and the Line

They were travelling in a hot-air balloon. When the circular circumference of the balloon crossed an electric power line, the balloon crashed, and its passengers were killed.

The Perfect Murder

Edward placed a tray on the edge of the kitchen table. He put some pans on one side of the tray and ice cubes on the other side. When the ice eventually melted, the weight of the pans caused the tray to fall off the table. The pans bounced on the floor and the alarm was activated. To the police, the tray, pans, and water looked to be part of the general disturbance in the kitchen.

The Sniper

He pours away the water and fills the bottle with gasoline from the car. He stuffs the handkerchief into the top of the bottle to make a Molotov cocktail. He waits until the sniper approaches the car and then lights the handkerchief before hurling the bottle at his attacker.

Fair Deal

The police arrested the dealer and charged her with murder.

The Cloth

The man who died was shot in a duel. The man who waved the cloth gave the signal that the two duelists could commence.

Bostonian

He was born in Boston, Massachusetts, in the early 18th century when it was still a British colony. He was British.

The Tree and the Axe

She bought a Christmas tree. After Christmas, she put it in the garden, and the next day she chopped it up.

Below Par

It was a nine-hole golf course.

School Friend

Joe's old school friend was a woman called Louise.

Sell More Beer

The management consultant noticed that the barman was leaving extra room in each glass. He told the bar owner to have the glasses filled up to the top!

The Lumberjacks

Joe uses his breaks to sharpen his axe.

The Clinch

Their braces were locked together.

Precognition

The lady was a postal worker delivering a registered letter addressed to Mrs. Turner.

Dud Car

Nova means "won't go" in Spanish.

Red Light

The teenagers were travelling on the road that crossed the road the police officer was on. They drove through a green light.

Nun-plussed

The nun was suffering from severe hiccups. The doctor examined her and told her she was pregnant. The shock cured her hiccups, but she ran out before he could explain that his "diagnosis" was only a ruse to rid her of the hiccups.

Confectionery Manufacturer

The workers are bees in a beehive.

The Painter

He had painted the walls at the art galleries.

Regular Arguments

They were acting in a play which involved a violent argument.

Beautiful Girls

He had the two beautiful girls tattooed on his arms.

Orange Trick

Put it under the table.

The Fall

He was on a roller coaster.

The Bookmark

The man argues that he can use the dollar bill itself as a bookmark, and then spend it whenever he likes.

Good-bye, Mother

The young woman was presented with the bill for the old lady's meal. The lady had assured the waiter, "My daughter will pay."

Steer Clear of the Banks

The man was disabled. He got out of his car and onto his wheelchair. He used the wheelchair to go up and down the main street.

A Hairy Story

She shaved her head!

By the River

The man was about to start a boat race by firing a starting pistol.

The Helicopter

The helicopter was hovering just over the helicopter landing pad on an oil platform out at sea.

Car in the River

The water in the river came up to the man's chest.

Pay Phone

She told the telephone company that people were making free international telephone calls because of a problem with the pay phone. They promptly sent someone to fix it.

The Typist

Typing eleven words per minute is going quite fast, if the language is Chinese!

Two Jugs

The jugs were full of frozen cubes of lemonade and milk. They stayed separate even when poured into the one large vat.

Speeding Ticket

In the very early days of motoring, the speed limit was 8 miles per hour.

Twin Trouble

Bob and Sam were born on the night that the clocks are set back for the summer. Bob was born at 1:45 a.m. Sam was born 30 minutes later. The clocks were set back one hour at 2 a.m., so Sam's official time of birth was 1:15 a.m.

Library Lunacy

The library was moving to new premises but had very little money for the move. By giving the borrowers extra time, it ensured that borrowers moved most of the books.

Elevator

The woman was from out of town and had heard stories of violence and muggings in the big city. She found herself alone in an elevator with a large, fearsome-looking man who had a big Alsatian dog. The man said, "Sit, Lady!"

The terrified woman sat down only to see the dog do the same. The man cheerfully helped her up and they had a laugh about the incident.

Fall of the Wall

The guards were bribed.

Smart Appearance

The mortuary had prepared Victor well for his funeral.

Dogs Home

He could only see half of the sign on the back of the truck because one door was open and the other closed. The full sign read "Dogson's Home Produce." It was a delicatessen's van.

Title Role

She got the title role in the movie "Rebecca." Rebecca does not appear anywhere in this movie.

Job Lot

The bricks he had bought were designed for building a chimney. They were all slightly curved and, consequently, of no use to the builder.

The Lifeboat

It was a wooden lifeboat. The wood swelled after two days at sea and sealed its own leaks.

Invaluable

The man stole a lottery ticket. It turned out to be a winning ticket for a big prize. If it had been a small prize, he could have claimed it safely and anonymously at any lottery shop. To claim a large prize he would have to report to the authorities. He did not know where the ticket had been bought. If the original owner went to the police, then it was likely the man could be identified as a thief and sent to prison. So he threw the ticket away.

The Crash

One of the two trucks was a car transporter carrying six brand-new cars.

Westward Ho!

(West) Bristol — Reading — London (East)

The two men walked to the railway station in Reading and boarded the train for Bristol at its western end. They walked to the restaurant car in the center of the train and had a long lunch. Then they continued walking east along the train, which arrived in Bristol.

40 Feet Ahead

The man walked around the Earth. Since he was walking on the surface of a sphere, his head, which was 6 feet farther away from the center of the sphere than his feet, travelled 2pi × 6 feet farther. (It can be argued that it is impossible to walk around the Earth, but this does not matter. Any walk of any distance on the surface of the Earth involves the same principle. A walk of 26,000 miles on the Earth's surface would mean that the man's head travelled about 40 feet farther than his feet.)

The Circular Table

She cuts out a piece of paper exactly the size of the table. She folds the paper in half twice, along any two diameters (by easily matching opposite sides of the circle). Where the two folds meet is the center. She then places the paper on top of the table.

T-Shirts

A law was introduced, making the wearing of seat belts compulsory for car drivers and passengers. Many Italians tried to circumvent the law. They wore the T-shirts in order to give the false impression that they were wearing seat belts.

Two Suitcases

The man is on his way to check or leave the baggage for storage. Now he only has to pay for one item.

The Nonchalant Police Officer

The police officer saw the incident on a TV screen in the window of a consumer electronics store.

Rare Event

The numbers of the year 1961 read the same when turned upside-down. This will not happen again until 6009.

Holy Orders

A child had released a helium-filled balloon in the church. It was high out of reach but clearly visible. The priest was going to shoot it down with an air gun.

Well-Dressed

If it was someone she wanted to invite in, she said she had just come in. If it was someone she did not want to invite in, she said she was just about to go out.

Kid Stuff

The expert believes that some drivers mistake children for adults and subconsciously assume that, because the figures are small, the children are farther away than they actually are.

The Two Drivers

This incident took place in Saudi Arabia in 1995. It is illegal for women to drive in Saudi Arabia. One driver was a man and the other a woman. The police officer arrested the woman, who was charged and convicted.

Keys in the Car

The man had already phoned his wife, who was 100 miles away, and persuaded her to drive to him with the spare set of keys. He does not want to have to explain to her that her journey was unnecessary and face her wrath.

The Hasty Robber

He was fleeing from the scene of the crime and failed to see a police officer with a radar gun. He was stopped for speeding and ultimately convicted of robbery.

How to Choose a Builder

He asked each builder to nominate an alternate in case he could not take up the contract. He gave the contract to the builder most often nominated as backup.

The Unlucky Gambler

The unlucky gambler had drawn a "ticket" bearing the number 6 ⅞ (the hat label with the size marked on it).

Brush-off

Amanda hangs up while she herself is speaking. She can subsequently claim they were disconnected.

The Code

The correct answer to "Ten" is "Three." The code is the number of letters in the first word.

Time of Arrival

When he came in, the boy had removed his boots and placed them on top of the morning paper.

Depressurization

The rattle he heard was a rattlesnake that had somehow got into the plane. By depressurizing the plane, he starved the snake of oxygen and it died. He was wearing an oxygen mask and survived.

A Solution of Paint

Samuel Plimsoll initiated a movement which led the British in 1875, and subsequently other nations, to draw a line, the Plimsoll line, on the hull of every cargo ship showing the maximum depth to which the ship could be loaded. Prior to this, many ships had sunk because they were overloaded.

Strange Reactions

They worked as testers in a chemical-testing factory. Joan was testing an onion substitute, while John was testing laughing gas.

Striking the Elephant

The man is playing billiards (or snooker or pool) with balls made of ivory. By pocketing a ball with his cue, he wins the match.

Gaze Away

The man was the King of England. Until recently, it was considered very bad manners to look directly at the monarch. People were expected to look down or away, and never in the King's face.

Desert

It was a very cold desert. He survived by eating snow or ice.

The Deadly Diamonds

The thief simply took the box, turned it upside-down, tilted it, and slid open the lid. The diamonds rolled out.

The Archaeologist

The ancient item was a dinosaur bone. When the professor's dog found the bone he took it out through the cat-door and buried it in the garden!

The Container

A ring.

Mutilation

He had committed a murder. His fingerprints had been found at the scene of the crime, but his identity was not yet known to the police. He dipped the ends of his fingers in acid to destroy his fingerprints.

Cowardly Act

During World War I, some soldiers in the trenches deliberately exposed their hands or feet during heavy gunfire in the hope of sustaining an injury that would gain them a discharge and so avoid the risk of death.

Fall of the Hall

The building was owned by the National Geological Society, although it had not been originally designed for them. Over the years, the society's collection of rock specimens grew and eventually the weight of the rocks caused the building to collapse.

The Cicada

It is believed that the 17-year life cycle gives an advantage because 17 is a prime number. Consequently, it is most unlikely that any predator would have a life cycle in synchronization with this cicada. If there were a large population of cicada one year and a consequent increase in predators, then the cicada offspring generation, which would emerge in 17 years, would not coincide with a large generation of predators because their life cycles would not be factors of 17.

Candy in Pocket

In 1945, Percy Le Baron Spencer, an engineer at Raytheon who was working on radar equipment, noticed that a candy in his pocket had melted. He correctly deduced that this was caused by microwave radiation that had agitated the molecules in the candy. Following this discovery, Raytheon designed and patented the world's first microwave oven.

Stringing Along

The man was taking part in a kite-flying competition. He glued tiny pieces of glass to his kite strings so that they would cut the strings of competitors' kites. He won the competition, but was subsequently disqualified.

The Painting

She said that this was the room where she meditated while standing on her head, and that she had hung it upside-down so she could view it as she meditated.

Mickey Mouse's Girlfriend

During the Battle of the Bulge in World War II, German soldiers speaking very good English and wearing American uniforms infiltrated the American forces to confuse and misdirect them. This question was designed to identify the impostors.

The Parcel

The parcel contained her husband's sandwiches, which he had forgotten to take to work. He worked in the lost-and-found office of the bus company.

The Suitcase and the Box

The man had just been released from prison. While there, he had caught and painstakingly trained a cockroach. It was kept in a little box and could do tricks. He went into a bar to celebrate his release and got the cockroach to do one of its tricks on the bar. He called to the bartender, "Hey, look at this." Whereupon the bartender killed it with a blow from his towel, saying, "That's the third one today!"

Third Place

The man was Charlie Chaplin. While on vacation he entered a Charlie Chaplin look-alike competition but he took third place!

The Missing Diamond

The thief had left a tape recorder in the room which recorded the sound of the man opening and closing the safe. From the number of clicks, the thief was able to work out the combination. (He could not tell whether to turn the dial left or right initially, so he tried them both.)

Paddle Your Own Canoe

This incident took place in Australia, where, at a certain time of year, the rains create a river that flows down a course and then eventually dries up. Effectively, the river is a body of water that moves from one point to another, then disappears.

Poor Impersonation

The heiress had a mannerism whereby she leaned her head to the left as she spoke. The actress rehearsed her gestures in front of a mirror, so she leaned her head to the right.

Doctor's Appointment

The woman explained that she was the telephone repairperson and had come to fix the phone. The new doctor had been lying about making the calls.

Creepy Crawlies

He asks the managers of his local cinema, bars, and community halls for the old cigarette ends, or butts, collected from containers. This debris they gladly give him in abundance, and he boils and strains the material to form a lethal nicotine-based insecticide which he uses to kill all the pests in his garden.

Sweet Wheat

Wheat pollinates by wind. The farmer is protecting his own future crops from contamination by inferior pollen from his neighbors' crops.

Three Notes

The woman was a traffic warden who wrote out three parking tickets. The bank robber had parked a stolen car which he intended to dump after the robbery, so he threw the ticket away. The tourist was returning to Bolivia shortly, so he threw his ticket away. The priest was sad because he would have to pay his fine.

Catching a Bullet

The first man fires the bullet vertically. The second man is standing at the top of a cliff. The bullet just reaches the top of its flight near the top of the cliff and it falls gently into the man's outstretched hand.

The problem can be restated so that the bullet is fired horizontally, in which case the solution is as follows:

A man fires a bullet from the back of a jet plane which is flying horizontally at the exact speed of the bullet and in the opposite direction to that of the bullet. Relative to the ground the bullet has no horizontal velocity. It would fall into the hand of a man standing under the plane at the point where the bullet was fired.

WALLY Test I Answers (p. 21)

1. Eight days. Each day he takes out one ear of corn and two squirrel ears!
2. The first triangle is larger—one with sides measuring 200, 300 and 400 cm. The triangle with sides measuring 300, 400 and 700 cm has an area of zero (It would be a straight line).
3. Halfway—after that, it is running out of the woods.
4. In total darkness none of them could see a thing.
5. Mount Everest.
6. On the head.
7. The president would remain president.
8. No candles burn longer—all candles burn shorter.
9. He had one large haystack.
10. Short.
11. A pound of feathers weighs more than a pound of gold. Gold is measured in Troy pounds, which weigh less than the regular Avoirdupois pounds in which items such as feathers would be weighed.
12. A bed.

WALLY Test II Answers (p. 32)

1. 1 and 17.
2. Bread.
3. Sixes, sixth, or sixty.
4. In England, it is not usual to bury people who are still alive.
5. One—after that, his stomach is not empty.

6. The Unfinished Symphony was written by Schubert.

7. Wrongly.

8. A hole.

9. You would be losing 45 cents. I gave you 30 cents in exchange for the three quarters.

10. 12.

WALLY Test III Answers (p. 64)

1. None.

2. It is best to take a photograph of a man with a camera.

3. All of them.

4. The window.

5. He drove in reverse.

6. Neither. The plane was over the Gulf of Mexico, so they both hit water.

7. Nine.

8. Most nuns use spoons.

9. To make the elevator move.

10. Lend me $13!

11. Time to get a new clock!

12. Two men, one of whom was a grandfather.

13. The archaeologist was right, of course. The coin had been found in a cloth which was carbon dated 200 BC.

14. a) white; b) water (most people say milk).

About the Authors

PAUL SLOANE was born in Scotland and grew up near Blackpool in the north of England. He studied engineering at Trinity Hall, Cambridge, and graduated with a first-class honors degree. While at Cambridge he met his wife, Ann, who is a teacher. They live in Camberley, England, with their three daughters.

Most of Paul Sloane's career has been in the computer industry, and he is currently the European vice president for a software company. He has always been an avid collector and creator of puzzles. His first book, *Lateral Thinking Puzzlers*, was published by Sterling in 1991. Paul Sloane has given speeches and radio talks on the topic of change management and lateral thinking.

DES MACHALE was born in County Mayo, Ireland, and is Associate Professor of Mathematics at University College in Cork. He was educated at University College, Galway, and the University of Keele in England. He and his wife, Anne, have five children.

The author of over thirty books, mostly of humor but also one on giving up smoking, Des MacHale has many interests including puzzles, geology, writing, broadcasting, films, photography, numismatics, and, of course, mathematics. He is currently working on several new projects.